What is Intergenerational Justice?

What is Intergenerational Justice?

Axel Gosseries

polity

First published in 2023 by Polity Press

Polity Press
65 Bridge Street
Cambridge CB2 1UR, UK

Polity Press
111 River Street
Hoboken, NJ 07030, USA

ISBN-13: 978-1-5095-2571-3
ISBN-13: 978-1-5095-2572-0 (pb)

A catalogue record for this book is available from the British Library.

Library of Congress Control Number: 2022941388

Typeset in 11 on 13pt Sabon
by Fakenham Prepress Solutions, Fakenham, Norfolk NR21 8NL
Printed and bound in Great Britain by CPI Group (UK) Ltd, Croydon

For further information on Polity, visit our website:
politybooks.com

Contents

Acknowledgments

Philosophy is a collective (and intergenerational) effort. My debt is huge to all those who had the generosity and patience to share their thoughts with me over the years on the issues discussed in this book. This includes the small community of scholars working on intergenerational justice, but also my close colleagues and students at Louvain University and at other academic institutions where I had the chance to go for research or teaching visits. I want to stress that I have been unable to do justice to all the great papers published on the topic, as this would have turned the book into an encyclopedia. I am sure that some of you will feel hurt by this lack of recognition. I hope that you will forgive me and understand that it merely reflects the lack of space allowed by a concise book like this one.

I had the great privilege of receiving insightful feedback on specific issues or full draft chapters from several friends and colleagues. They include Pierre André, Kim Angell, Chris Armstrong, Arshak Balayan, Ludvig Beckman, Greg Bognar, Eric Boot, Eric Brandstedt, John Broome, Paula Casal, Louis Chauvel, Steve Gardiner, Anca Gheaus, Inigo Gonzalez Ricoy, Robert Goodin, Jonathan Hoffmann,

Kasper Lippert-Rasmussen, Catriona McKinnon, Tim Meijers, Patrick Meyfroidt, Soren Mitgaard, Andreas Mogensen, Gregory Ponthière, Raffaele Rodogno, Liam Shields, Adam Swift, Vincent Vandenberghe, Christophe Vandeschrick, Philippe Van Parijs, Alexandru Volacu, Nicholas Vrousalis, and Andrew Williams. To some extent, they are the co-authors of this book, even if I'm happy to take full responsibility for the many remaining imperfections.

I also had the chance of presenting earlier versions of some of the chapters over the last few years in front of various audiences at seminars and crash courses, including at Aarhus (AU/AIAS), Amsterdam (UvA), Barcelona (UB), Bayreuth (UB), Bergen (UiB), Braga (UM), Budapest (MTA), Burgos (UBU), Campinho (FPP), Coimbra (UC), Copenhagen (AAU), Frankfurt (Normative Orders), Hamburg (UH), Leuven (KULeuven), Lisbon (Gulbenkian/UNL), London (LSE), Luxembourg (MPI), Manchester (MANCEPT), Marseille (IMéRA), Monaco (AOMF), Oviedo (UO), Paris (UPEC), Pisa (SUSP), Riga (SSE), Rome (LUISS), Stockholm (IFFS), Tbilisi (TSU), Trondheim (NTNU), and Yerevan (YSU). What you will read owes a lot to the minds and hospitality of those audiences too.

Work on this book has benefited from funding from various institutions. The FNRS is definitely the first one to mention, having been my main employer for a quarter of a century. It has always left me an incredible amount of freedom. Let me also mention specific FNRS research grants that allowed me to spend time at Stockholm's Institute for Future Studies (2016–18) and Aarhus's Institute of Advanced Studies (2019). In addition, I benefited from research budgets from Louvain University's ARC "SAS Pensions" project and from various other institutions including Stockholm's Institute for Future Studies. Thanks to them for their precious support.

At Polity, I would like to thank especially Julia Davies, George Owers, and Fiona Sewell for their support and patience. Also, two anonymous referees wrote invaluable comments and suggestions on an earlier version of this manuscript. They all gave me the motivation and the space to express myself in the best possible way. Thanks for this!

I owe a last word to my friends and my close family. Writing this book has taken a lot of my energy. Without your support, I would not have managed to complete it. Besides Maria and Alicia, I owe a special mention to my Dad, who was certainly the most impatient among them to see this book come to life. Thanks for your soft and tireless smiling pressure, Dad!

Introduction

Key environmental and social challenges often exhibit a salient generational dimension. Climate change concerns standardly point to our duties to future generations or to those resulting from past emissions. Nuclear waste management requires a long-term perspective, anticipating burdens for centuries ahead. Worries about pension equity and sustainability typically stress questions of fairness across coexisting generations. The 2016 Brexit vote raised concerns of democratic legitimacy framed in generational terms, the young having to live for longer with the consequences of a vote that they disagreed with. As to the 2019–22 COVID crisis, the saliency of the age criterion in access to intensive care units (ICUs) and vaccines, as well as the differential vulnerability across ages to both COVID and anti-COVID measures, led many to wonder whether our youth had been unjustly sacrificed.

Generational concerns cannot simply be swept aside. They are practically significant and often philosophically sticky. They also connect with issues of existential threats, with concerns about the very continuation of humankind. One assumption of this book is that explicit philosophical thinking can help us grasp the conceptual and normative issues at stake and guide us toward fair solutions. We will straddle conceptual and normative territories. This will allow us to formulate and defend normative claims about what we owe each other as members of different generations. Changing society requires lucidity on natural and social facts, inventiveness on means, and a lot of work, courage, and political determination, but also a sense of what our means and goals should be. Spelling out the latter requires mastering a minimally rich repertoire to address the complexity of justice issues that pervade such challenges. Robust policy requires clear directions. Democratic policy requires a citizenry properly equipped to reflect upon and articulate its intuitions about what intergenerational justice is about. Philosophical clarification is one of the necessary steps in that direction.

Hence, this book on generations and justice is intended for philosophers and non-philosophers alike. It builds on work by philosophers over the last decades.[1] It focuses on the present and the future, less on our relationship with the past. It will not discuss measurement methods or alternative indicators to gross domestic product (GDP).[2] Nor will it provide up-to-date figures about whether the next generations can be expected to be worse off than us or whether some generations among us have been sacrificed. Yet it bears on these questions in important ways. It will explore whether what we owe the future is a matter of justice at all. It will discuss whether justice requires that the next generations be better off than us. It will look into how to assess whether a generation is doing better than another. It will touch on how institutional design may contribute to intergenerational fairness.

Silence and diversion

Engaging with generations reminds us of the fragility of our existence. We navigate between predecessors and successors, like tiny paragraphs of an open narrative in the writing. These relations confront us with philosophical puzzles. We are facing the possibility of strong duties toward beings that we may be unable to harm in a meaningful sense. We are expected to divide cakes without knowing how many guests will join us and what their tastes will be. We owe each other objects and actions along a time dimension that exhibits irreversibility.

In devoting time to philosophical explorations, we should neither lose sight of their real-life relevance, nor be naive about widespread rhetorical uses of the generational framing. Caution is needed on the latter, for two reasons that I will label "silence" and "diversion." Saying a few words about this from the outset will allow us to proceed without undue skepticism or unnecessary misunderstandings.

The "silence" idea refers to citizens, activists, and politicians invoking *absent generations* in support of their views, whatever the latter may be. They use phrases such as "we owe *x* to the future" or "we owe *x* to our ancestors," especially in circumstances in which arguments are hard to produce. Expressing concern for currently absent generations tends to signal noble, other-regarding intentions. Yet actual intentions may not always be so. Such phrases might instead be used in some cases to put disagreeing parties in an uncomfortable position. For dissenting may be read by some as a sign of indifference to other generations, rather than as a token of disagreement about *what* we owe the past or the future. More importantly, absent generations are silent: never do we come across dead or future demonstrators upholding "not in my name" banners. Hence, phrases invoking absent generations may sometimes be taking advantage of the silence of absent people in whose name policies are advocated. And they may also sometimes aim at trying to silence dissenters who disagree on our interpretation of what we owe the future. While intergenerational concerns make sense, we should always remain conscious of perverse uses of such concerns.

The other word of caution has to do with the worry that framing things in generational terms can serve as a "diversion" to reduce pressure on fighting injustice between genders, racial groups, or social classes, or even as a way of justifying furthering such injustices. Diversion may be worrisome in several ways. One can be concerned about the fact that focusing on generational differences may distract us from addressing what some consider to be much larger differences, for instance between social classes. Yet one can also worry about the fact that generational equity may be used to attack social rights – for example, in pension or health care – with the effect of deepening the gap between social classes even further.[3]

It is likely that generational framing is often used with such a diversionary purpose. Yet I am not prejudging at this stage about the relationship between the generational dimension and other dimensions of justice, such as global justice or gender justice. I will not assume that intergenerational justice concerns should be given more weight than global justice or gender justice concerns, for instance. I will also not assume that intergenerational injustices tend, as a matter of fact, to be larger than, for instance, class or racial injustices. And I will not assume that promoting intergenerational justice in specific policies will automatically contribute to furthering justice along other dimensions. In fact, the possibility of such a convergence depends in part on how we understand generational concerns, an issue to which I now turn.

Generation: two meanings (among others)

What do we mean by "generation"? Focusing on intergenerational justice is undoubtedly driven by an interest in how time relates to justice. It expresses a concern about justice between individuals that are located at different moments in history. It differentiates situations in which their existences overlap from situations in which they don't. It explores what follows from the fact that investment in technology requires time, or from the fact that the passage of time transforms individuals. And yet the relation between time and intergenerational justice is a complex one, as is that between space/territory and global justice. Some issues of justice for which time is central do not necessarily involve individuals from different generations. This is so when a theory of justice integrates the notion of "fresh starts" or cares about fairness between slow and fast people.[4] While justice across time and justice between generations overlap, they do not fully coincide.

Referring to justice "between generations" rather than, for instance, to "justice between individuals across generations" may also suggest that the value of a generation is irreducible to the value of its members, or even that the former trumps the latter. This may echo the independent – and sometimes superior – value ascribed to nations by some philosophical nationalists. Relatedly, referring to justice "between generations" could also suggest that generations should be treated as black boxes, ignoring "intragenerational" – or rather "non-generational" – injustices. It could even be read as focusing on generations that have a strong sense of self-identity and/or demonstrate especially strong vintage effects that distinguish them from one another.

None of this is implied here. I take "intergenerational justice" as meaning "injustices between individuals from different generations." I do not assume that non-generational injustices are morally less significant – or factually smaller – than intergenerational ones. Nor do I imply that generations matter more than the sum of their members. Nor should intergenerational justice disregard non-generational injustices. Nor do we necessarily need a sociologically rich notion of generation to proceed. The generational dimension is "just" one angle through which to look at injustices between individuals – not an insignificant one at all, yet one among significant others.

Now, to understand what I positively mean by "generation," we ought to contrast two meanings of the word: "age group" and "birth cohort."[5] While morally significant, this is a tricky distinction to grasp and use for several reasons, confusion pervading both across the social sciences and in public debate. The tight interrelation between the two realities also contributes to rendering intergenerational relations special.

An age group is a group of individuals that includes all the people who fell, fall, or will have fallen within a given age range – for instance being a teenager – *when* they did, do, or will do. Aristotle – my amazing Greek colleague – and Jeanne Calment – the French supercentenarian – were both part of the age group "teenagers" during ten years of their life. This is true regardless of whether one of them died at 62 whereas the other died at 122, or of the fact that one lived in the fourth century BC whereas the latter lived across the nineteenth and twentieth centuries. When we focus on the young Aristotle or the young Jeanne Calment, we look at them "as teenagers."

In contrast, a birth cohort is a group of individuals including all those who were born within a given period of time, typically one or two decades. For instance, the birth cohort "Millennials" includes all those born between 1980 and 2000, *all along* their lives. "Birth" is key in the phrase "birth cohort" (or "birth-period group"). In a single-generation world in which all would be born on the same date and all would have exactly the same longevity, we all would be part of the same birth cohort *and* of the same age group at each moment in time. However, our actual world is one of asynchronous births and deaths, a world in which birth cohorts follow one another and in which not all of us reach the same age at the same time.

Hence, the words "young adults" (age group) and "Millennials" (birth cohort) point to distinct ways of dividing up human populations. While the lucky among us will successively belong to several age groups – children, teenagers, adults, elderly – all of us, regardless of how lucky we are after our birth, will be part of a single birth cohort and be stuck with it. Also, the number of live members of an age group may exhibit ups and downs, through fluctuations in natality, longevity, or mobility. In contrast, the number of live members of a birth cohort reaches its peak as soon as we reach the end of the reference birth period. From then on, it starts declining until the birth cohort dies away. From the year 2000 onward, the population size of Millennials started its decline. In contrast with age groups, birth cohorts are mortals.

Four illustrations

The "birth cohort/age group" distinction is difficult to use. Both notions involve the passage of an identically indexed time that runs within an individual's life (successive age groups) or unfolds along humankind's journey (successive birth cohorts). Let me clarify the meaning and significance of this distinction for justice through four examples.

Our first example is climate change. Global warming raises clear issues of justice between *birth cohorts*. Did those that turned adult by 1990 act in a climatically fair manner toward the next generations? Are we putting in the necessary effort to reach a climate that is fair toward those who will come into existence in a century? Besides this cohortal dimension, global warming also raises issues of justice between age groups, for instance to the extent that elderly people tend to be more vulnerable to heat waves.

Consider, then, fairness in retirement pension schemes as a second example. Whenever we express concern about the ability of a pension scheme to adequately cover elderly people's basic needs, we are defending a certain view about justice between age groups. Similarly, worries about not overburdening the active population as providers of pension benefits imply assumptions about what one age group owes another. In contrast, when we adjust retirement age or the level of pension benefits to the evolution of life expectancy, we may aim at spreading the costs of demographic change across various birth cohorts, assuming perhaps that none of them should bear a larger proportion of the associated burden. Similarly, when some invoke the idea that each cohort should get back in pension benefits no less than it has put into the system through contributions,[6] they are concerned about birth cohorts too, albeit with a different idea of justice in mind.

Education policies are our third example. What kind of education we owe our children clearly raises issues of justice between *age groups*. How much of their budget should adults invest in their children's education? How far is it acceptable to act paternalistically toward children, imposing on them compulsory education or prohibiting them from working? Should elementary schools be seen primarily as a safe space protecting a precious sphere of childhood or, rather, mostly as an instrument to begin forming future professionals? Or should access to education be cheaper for young people than for adults? These questions are clearly about what we owe age groups.

Yet issues of justice between birth cohorts also arise in education. For instance, we will see in chapter 3 that asking ourselves about the kinds of preferences and values (if any) that should be taught to the next generation is key to justice between birth cohorts. Whether preserving pieces of heritage for the remote future will turn out to be valuable may also depend on whether we make sure to transmit to the future the ability to value such heritage or the technology to understand, use, or fix it. Similarly, if we exhaust easy-to-use natural resources, whether this is morally acceptable depends on "resources–technology" substitutability. And again, transferring substitutive technology to the next birth cohort requires educating its members to make sure they can benefit from it.

Our last example is the COVID-19 crisis. Age played a central role in our initial responses to it. Yet pointing to age does not necessarily entail that we merely care about age groups. We began facing the crisis under the assumption that age was a significant indicator of COVID-19 vulnerability. In many countries, we gave priority to the young in access to intensive care and to the elderly in access to vaccines. Such priorities were in fact driven mostly by efficiency concerns in access to health care across different age groups.

Yet the cohortal dimension was far from absent. Consider the worry that we may have sacrificed our youth. Young people were the least vulnerable to the virus and strongly affected by measures such as lockdowns. The idea of "sacrificing our youth" may primarily reflect a cohortal concern: the fear that they may end up having had a worse destiny than ours by the end of their life, due to scarring effects associated with COVID measures. I am not saying here that the "sacrificing our youth" claim is right. I am simply claiming that it is best understood as one of justice between birth cohorts.

Cohortal primacy

I stressed the need to distinguish "birth cohorts" from "age groups" for the purpose of justice. This book focuses on the former, for reasons of space, but also due to some *primacy* of justice between birth cohorts over justice between age groups.[7] By "primacy," I do not mean that there is no room for independent concerns of justice between age groups. Rather, I mean that while a theory of intergenerational justice involving no independent concern for age groups is conceivable, the reverse – i.e. a theory of intergenerational justice involving no independent concern for birth cohorts – would be implausible. Here are two considerations supporting such cohortal primacy.

First, there is the idea of justice between "entire lives" – "over lifetimes" – and its implications. The core claim shared by any version of the "entire-life" (or "lifetime") view – be it radical or moderate – is that fairness between members of two different generations *cannot* be meaningfully assessed without considering how each of them is likely to fare *over her entire life.*

The idea is that age-based differential entitlements will frequently remain unproblematic *if* they do not worsen entire-life inequalities. Some support teenager disenfranchisement in part by stressing that neighboring generations were or will be subject to the same temporary disenfranchisement. In a non-negligible set of cases, age-based differential treatment *will not* lead to differential treatment over people's lifetime. Sometimes, age-based differential treatment even *reduces* inequalities over entire lives. Allocating a vital organ to the young may contribute to *reducing* the gap between long-lived and short-lived persons. In addition, if we need to *choose* between reducing unfair inequalities at specific points in time *or* reducing unfair inequalities over people's entire lives, the "entire-life" view gives priority to the latter.

Of course, a theory of justice between age groups does not need to reject *every* synchronic inequality between two age groups either. Such a theory could even give some weight to comparisons over entire lives. However, the latter seem more at home with a cohortal approach because, although it is possible to define what age groups owe each other while endorsing the lifetime view, it seems less meaningful to engage in fairness-inquiring cohortal comparisons *without* endorsing a lifetime perspective. One will be inclined to compare two cohorts over what they ended up having enjoyed and suffered by the end of their entire lives. One might be less willing to compare two cohorts through the exclusive prism of how they fared during the first ten decades of adulthood, for instance, regardless of the rest of their lives. In addition, if our conception of justice between age groups takes the lifetime intuition on board, the cohortal approach might end up capturing many of the concerns that an independent view on age group justice may express. This is so whenever age-based differential treatment is mainly problematic to the extent that it translates into differential treatment over complete lives.

The second consideration supporting cohortal primacy hinges on the relative *magnitude* of the intergenerational transfers at stake. Let me define *descending* transfers as forward-oriented ones, running from us to the next generation(s). In contrast, *ascending* transfer(s) are backward-oriented ones, running from us to the previous generation(s). While the world of birth cohorts may seem more one-directional at first sight, bi-directionality definitely arises in the world of age groups. Taking care of our elderly parents or teaching our teenagers involves interactions between age groups in both directions.

Now, even if we limit interactions between age groups to the overlap, descending transfers are arguably *larger* than ascending transfers. Merely looking at state-based social transfers may leave us with the impression that we are living in pro-elderly societies, in which ascending intergenerational transfers between age groups are larger than descending ones. However, once we add cash and care transfers that are family-run, namely those that are not channeled through the state, the magnitude of social investments in children may in fact end up exceeding transfers to the elderly.[8] Even then, the extent to which they exceed pro-elderly transfers may not be massive.

This contrasts with birth cohorts. Because of time's arrow and the inaccessibility associated with the death of our ancestors, we don't generally have heavy *ascending* duties of distributive justice. In contrast, if we assume that duties of justice toward birth cohorts located down the line beyond the overlap make sense, they extend far into the future and involve numerous potential beneficiaries. This suggests a stronger asymmetry between ascending and descending duties in the realm of *birth cohorts* than in that of *age groups*.

From there, we can move to the final step. We owe respect, care, education, etc. to our children as an age group. Yet we owe them more than that as a birth cohort. We also owe them a "stock" of valuable resources "inherited" from nature – we will come back to this – as well as massive cultural resources resulting from the cumulated work of all our predecessors. It includes mineral resources, natural biodiversity, deep and rich topsoil, institutional solutions, engineering technologies, rich languages, musical styles, etc. Such resources go beyond what we owe our children *as an age group*, and are arguably of a larger magnitude. We owe more to our children than what we owe them *as children*. We also owe them resources not just for themselves, but to enable them to pass them on to their own children, grandchildren, and beyond. Descending transfers dominate ascending ones. And descending transfers toward the next generation as a birth cohort *include* and *exceed* those that we owe them as an age group. This is why I will focus primarily on birth cohorts.

The overlap

Policy issues often involve dimensions of justice *both* between birth cohorts and between age groups. I will focus on the cohortal one here. I will now clarify the relationship between the "birth cohort vs. age group" distinction and the "overlapping vs. non-overlapping" distinction, stressing the latter's significance.

Our lives and those of adjacent generations overlap: they are partly – yet not fully – coextensive in time. One could be tempted to adopt the following starting point: when it comes to overlapping generations, we would be dealing with issues of justice between age groups, whereas in non-overlapping generations contexts, issues would be those of justice between birth cohorts. Yet this would be a misleading starting point, for two reasons.

First, while issues of justice between age groups mainly arise in an overlapping context, they do not exclusively do so. When focusing on justice between age groups, we usually ask what their members owe each other in terms of care or cash, given the different and often complementary characteristics associated with age (physical, affective, intellectual). Yet it is not meaningless to ask, for instance, what current retirees owe children *in general*, including future children that they will never coexist with. This is so when they vote on issues related to children's rights, including on resources targeted at children, be it investment in future playgrounds or in future schools. Hence, issues of justice between age groups may arise even beyond the overlap. Second – and more significantly – our four examples above show that serious issues of justice between birth cohorts arise at the overlap too.

In fact, theorizing the role of the overlap in a theory of justice between birth cohorts is essential. Here are four ways in which it matters. The existence of an overlap may offer solutions to serious problems faced by non-overlapping relationships. Our discussion of the non-identity problem in chapter 1 will illustrate this. Moreover, the way we conceive of the coexistence of our duties toward the next generation and our duties toward more remote future generations is also key. We will see in chapters 1 and 2 that our duties toward the remote future can be reframed to some extent as duties toward the next generation, through paying due attention to the latter's own duties toward its follower generations.

In addition, we depend on intermediary generations, including overlapping ones, to pass on resources to remote future ones, as we find ourselves in a time-locked situation, unable to reach the remote future ourselves. We thus need to articulate the possibility of direct duties to the future with our inability to fully fulfil them ourselves, namely to pass material and immaterial resources directly to the remote future. If we plant a jujube tree meant to live for 3,000 years, we need to count on intermediary generations to take care of it. If we value a culture for the freedom of its poetry, its hospitality, or its self-deprecating sense of humor, and if we manage to capture this as a matter of intergenerational duties, we need to rely on intermediary birth cohorts for such valuable traits to be passed on to remote future generations.

Finally, another angle is provided by public-interest climate litigation. Plaintiffs in court typically face the legal constraint of "standing" when considering taking on board not-yet-born plaintiffs. Yet it has been a key strategy for climate activists to rely instead on young plaintiffs who already coexist with us. They are typically involved as representatives of their age group *and* of their birth cohort, their additional life expectancy extending much further into the future than that of adult plaintiffs. This stresses the centrality of the overlap for justice between birth cohorts, including – yet not exclusively – through its role in rendering meaningful obligations toward more remote generations.

Having stressed the overlap's importance for inter-generational justice, let me return to non-overlapping generations, involving persons who will never coexist. Because the latter setting faces several challenges, fixing one will not be enough. This is why the set of "solutions" to the non-identity problem proposed in chapter 1 will not suffice to put non-overlapping generations aside for the rest of the book. In chapter 3, the fact that we do not know today about the preferences of future people is a serious challenge too. In chapter 4, the fact that current people were not present in the past is a real issue for any rectificatory claim grounded on historical injustice. And the uncertainty about whether there will be people in the future matters for the social discount rate debate too. In chapter 5, the current voicelessness and toothlessness of future people will be key to our concerns about the possibility of intergenerationally legitimate decisions.

Hence, while a theory of intergenerational justice should integrate both overlapping and non-overlapping generations settings, one should pay special attention to the following two aspects. On the one hand, philo-sophical issues raised by the absence of overlap do not reduce to those that drive the non-identity problem. This is why I continue beyond chapter 1 to look into other challenges arising in non-overlap settings. Also, taking non-overlapping generations seriously is not primarily motivated by giving a priority to philosophical puzzlement. It mainly feeds on the observation that the majority of generations to which we potentially owe duties of justice do not overlap with us. This echoes the fact that, in the realm of global justice, only a tiny minority of the countries to which we owe duties are in fact bordering our territory. On the other hand, philosophical issues of justice between cohorts do not become self-evident once we concentrate on overlapping generations. Each and every one of the four chapters following the first one illustrates this.

Is justice really the issue?

We now have a better grasp of the notion of generations. A few words are needed about what I mean by justice. Let me begin with the idea of distributive justice, which will be at the core of this book. Various forms of egalitarianism instantiate this distributive idea. And here, we are interested in distributive justice between generations. How does it differ from related concepts?

Consider first the complex "ethics/justice" distinction. A common view is that obligations of justice refer to a *subset* of our ethical obligations, namely those that the state is entitled to enforce on its citizens. This is typically how libertarians, being especially sensitive to possible abuses of state power, tend to frame things. For instance, they limit the tax base available to fund redistributive transfers. Even utilitarians may have something to say about duties for which enforceability would be desirable and duties for which it wouldn't, admittedly on more contingent grounds. Importantly enough, one can only conclude that a set of duties is minimalist or undemanding if one considers the full package of both enforceable and non-enforceable duties. For one might very well endorse the view that legally enforceable duties should be kept to a minimum (because of a certain conception of the role of the state), while defending a very extensive set of non-enforceable duties.

How does this translate into the intergenerational realm? One issue is whether the material *inability* of a state to enforce something entails that it would not be *entitled to* enforce it, were it able to do so, and that related duties of justice would simply transform into "merely" ethical ones. This is a situation that we come across in the case of failed states. The intergenerational context beyond the overlap is also challenging in this respect as enforcement tends to require coexistence – an issue to which I return in chapter 5. Hence, future people with whom we will never coexist are unable to enforce duties on us. Does this entail that we don't have duties *of justice* toward them? Not if we consider it sufficient that the state is *currently* able to enforce duties to the future on its current citizens. For the question of whether some duties should be enforceable on citizens arises as soon as there is an authority to enforce them, regardless of whether this authority is future or present. Hence, I will assume that the issue of enforceable duties of intergenerational justice arises within and also beyond the overlap.[9] We will see that besides the challenge posed by our *inability to enforce* duties beyond the overlap, another challenge to the possibility of harm-based duties of justice beyond the overlap arises out of the so-called "non-identity" problem – to which we return extensively in chapter 1.

Consider next the "legitimacy/justice" distinction. Strikingly enough, late-eighteenth-century thinkers such as Thomas Jefferson or Nicolas de Condorcet framed inter-generational concerns in terms other than justice. They were drafting constitutions. Their concern was rather about generational *sovereignty* or intergenerational *legitimacy*. Their worry was not so much that we might leave a world to the future that is worse than ours. It rather had to do with the fact that constitutional rigidity may illegitimately limit the free exercise of political power by future generations. This concern about imposing our say on the future somehow echoes the concerns expressed by some about the insufficient voting weight of the young in deciding about 2016 Brexit. Legitimacy is about fair procedures, about democratic decision-making. Distributive justice is about the distribution of well-being, resources, etc. For those who accept this divide and don't endorse overinclusive definitions of justice and legitimacy, a decision can be distributively just while being democratically illegitimate, and conversely. Both justice and legitimacy face challenges in the intergenerational context. I will focus on the former in this book, even though I will return to the latter in chapter 5.

In a sense, I have first stressed challenges to the *possibility* of a justice-based account, be it through referring to challenges to enforceability or to the "non-identity" challenge. What the reference to legitimacy brings is a potential attack on the *significance* of a justice-focused approach. The worry is not so much that justice would not apply. It is rather that it would be missing the main point. Legitimacy-focused people might call for rather rethinking the conditions of legitimate decision-making in a context of massive absenteeism from those in the past and in the future. And they might be joined by sustainability scholars who might want to stress that the core issues we are facing are of sustainability rather than justice. I will return to this in chapter 2. At this stage, I simply claim that concerns of justice between birth cohorts, including beyond the overlap, are both meaningful and significant. I hope that this book will provide ample evidence for this. Of course, I am not denying that careful distinctions are required between different dimensions of justice (rectificatory, distributive, relational, ...), between justice and sustainability, justice and legitimacy, and so forth. And I hope that this book will also shed light on this.

Road map

Let me end with a road map. The book is divided into five chapters. The first four are about justice while the fifth is concerned with legitimacy. In chapter 1, I respond to the question "*Can we* have duties of justice to the future?" whereas in the three subsequent chapters I look at "*What are* our duties of justice to the future?" Chapter 1 deals with a troubling issue called the "non-identity" problem. I explain what the problem is and why it is significant. And then I propose three possible elements of a solution to the problem.

Chapters 2 and 3 are two companion chapters. One deals with intergenerational justice's *principle* (or criterion), whereas the other deals with its *metrics* (or currency). If you think that justice is, for instance, about "maximizing the total amount of opportunity for well-being in society," your principle is "maximizing the total amount" and your metrics is "opportunity for well-being." In chapter 2, I explore four possible principles. I unveil their logics and implications. I explore alternative ways of framing them and their connection with the idea of sustainability. In chapter 3, I address some key challenges associated with the fact that a metrics of intergenerational justice needs to take the following two facts seriously: we don't know what the preferences of future people will turn out to be *and* we partly have control over the content of such future preferences.

Chapter 4 explores climate justice as an example, bridging it with the previous chapters. This chapter discusses the significance of historical emissions, the defensibility of climate degradation, the idea of early effort, and the meanings of the social discount rate. Chapter 5 looks at the extent to which intergenerational legitimacy is a meaningful goal to pursue. And it explores the implications for institutional design. A short conclusion closes the book.

When contemplating the beauties and disasters of our world, this book is likely to leave passionate readers frustrated. I have left an array of issues aside. Readers have limited time. More importantly, modesty is key. While the intergenerational dimension is significant, it should not hide other dimensions of justice. While philosophical exploration is precious, it remains irresolute or silent on many issues, and insights from other disciplines are fundamental. While theory is powerful, courageous human action is ultimately needed to change the world. Hopefully, it will be self-conscious action, enriched by insights from careful observation and deliberation, including of a philosophical nature, and motivated by the common good.

1

Can we act *unjustly* toward the future?

There is a strong sense in which the ability of humankind to deeply change the world and the future has increased over the last decades, which led to calling our times the Anthropocene. It seems to follow that our ability to *harm* the future has risen accordingly and that this entails a rising responsibility. Yet, like a grain of sand in the gears, the "non-identity" problem, unveiled by Parfit in the late 1970s, has kept the philosophical community busy ever since.[1] For this problem questions the possibility of meaningfully characterizing our actions as potentially harmful to the future. In a sense, work by philosophers on the "non-identity" problem is akin to that of the biomedical community facing a new pathogen. The fact that a pathogen has been newly discovered does not mean that it cannot be dangerous. Instead of denying its existence or importance, we should try to precisely assess its nature, implications, and possible remedies.

I will present and defend three main strategies to address the non-identity problem. They are partly complementary. Each of them relies on different assumptions about the justice–harm nexus. Each seeks to show that while the non-identity problem is serious, it does not render the idea of significant obligations to the future meaningless. The chapter is structured as follows. I first present the non-identity problem. Next, I discuss the link between harm and justice. I then move to the three "rescue" strategies. I explore whether relying on a *new grammar* – namely, alternative concepts of harm – can offer a solution. I then present the *containment* option. It sticks to an ordinary concept of harm, while calling for rethinking the nature of our intergenerational obligations. Finally, I explore the *severance* alternative. Here, the idea is to free concerns of justice to the future from heavily relying on the concept of harm.

Let me add two words of caution. First, having gained an initial grasp of the non-identity problem, unfamiliar readers might feel cheated and react with disbelief or even irritation. They might think: "I can't believe this! Philosophers have made it up! How can they possibly spend time at all on such a far-fetched problem while some of Earth's fundamentals are collapsing?" I hope to show that, while surprising, the problem is serious. This holds regardless of whether one thinks that too much intellectual energy has been spent on it and too little on other philosophical and non-philosophical problems. Because acting meaningfully matters, we cannot just dismiss it. Second, some may argue that the fact that the non-identity problem threatens the meaningfulness of duties to the future is rather good news. It should make us feel relieved and light-hearted, whatever we do. It should be seen as a cure rather than a pathogen. Anyone with a lasting sense of strong duties to the future would resist such a conclusion, though.

The non-identity problem

What does the non-identity problem consist in? By way of illustration, consider the idea of *optimal age of reproduction*.[2] It stresses the timing dimension of the non-identity problem. In many societies, social pressure or even legal restrictions – such as sexual majority ages or lower/upper age limits for medically assisted reproduction

– push people not to reproduce outside an age window. This may rest on several justifications. We may want to guarantee proper sexual consent or limit health-care costs. But we may also be imposing such age restrictions out of concern for the interest of the to-be-born child. Aren't children better off with parents equipped with sufficient judgment abilities and with sufficient additional longevity to be able to accompany them into adulthood? Such justifications actually face the non-identity problem. Had the person decided to conceive a child at another age, it would have been another child, not this one. Hence, for *this* very child, this is the best possible life. In what sense could this person then meaningfully claim to have been harmed, or even wronged? This is the challenge.

The non-identity problem has to do with a trivial fact, one of puzzling and potentially radical consequences. Let me begin by dissipating a few possible confusions. The expression "non-identity" *does not* refer to the mere fact that future people are likely to qualitatively differ from us, whether in being more short-sighted, fatter, or less red haired. *Neither* does it single out the likely fact that the preferences of future people might differ from ours, whether in being more passionate about rap music, more sensitive to gender bias, or less keen on natural environments. *Nor* does the expression merely point to the fact that the goods – natural and cultural resources – at the disposal of future generations are likely to differ from ours. The focus is not merely on whether future people's lungs will be more resistant to pollution, whether they will form weaker preferences for clean air, whether their air will be more polluted, or whether they will benefit from social arrangements well adjusted to episodes of air pollution.

Instead, when we talk about "non-identity," we are in fact referring to the *interaction* between someone's internal (e.g. one's legs) and external (e.g. one's bike) resources and a person's *numerical identity*. What does this mean? When we consider "identical twins," they are identical in a qualitative, "type" sense, at least genetically. And yet, since they are two separate persons, they are non-identical in another, numerical, "token" sense. Consider now the interaction between a person's numerical identity and her qualitative identity, the latter referring here to the state of her *internal* resources only (such as the state of her lungs). In an ordinary setting, one can modify a person's physical features (e.g. turn her black hair red) or the content of her preferences (e.g. convince her to prefer red hair) while claiming that she still remains the same person, in the numerical sense. In contrast, in a non-identity setting, you cannot merely modify certain features of a person's condition, because the only way of doing so requires bringing *another* person into existence instead. In such a context, the only way in which we can ensure a person having red hair rather than black hair is to bring *another* person (with black hair) into existence instead. The type change requires a token change. Improvement can only be achieved through selection. In a non-identity context, qualitative change cannot be achieved without numerical change. In such a specific context, *changing a person* necessarily implies *changing person*, i.e. bringing about a different person.

What is true of the person's internal resources is also true of her *external* circumstances. In a normal setting, if Pablo lives in a polluted environment, it is possible to improve Pablo's environment without the need for Pablo to be substituted with Marta. In a non-identity setting, adopting a policy to clean up the environment will also entail that it is Marta rather than Pablo who will be born. *Changing a person's environment* necessarily implies *changing person*.

At this stage, the reader may remain skeptical. Do any real-world situations actually fit such descriptions? What is the underlying story? As a matter of fact, most of our policies have an effect on the *timing* of people's actions. For instance, energy, employment, education, and transportation policies influence when people get up, the time they spend fetching food, when they are back home, and ... when they make love. The last fact explains the unintended and indirect impact of non-reproductive policies on *who* will be born. A lot of non-reproduction-related policies affect the timing of our reproductive acts. As a result, they also affect the identity of who will come to existence. This is the compelling *starting point* of the non-identity problem. We still need to understand how that can lead to a *problem*. For some authors, it threatens no less than the very possibility of obligations *of justice* to the future.[3] We will show that it is not necessarily the case.

In order to grasp things further, consider three other types of directly reproductive choices – besides our "optimal age" example. First case: *human cloning*. It involves a direct connection between a policy choice and the identity of who will be born. It also helps us to clearly separate qualitative from numerical identity issues. People can be concerned about cloning humans for various reasons.[4] One of them rests with the concern that cloning involves something wrong *toward the new person* that results from the cloning exercise – hereinafter "the clone." Yet, in the absence of cloning, the clone would not have existed. How can we claim that this life is worse than an alternative life *for this person* if this is the only possible one for her? How could an action possibly be regarded as harmful to someone if that action is necessary for *that person* to come to existence? Cloning confronts us with two competing claims, each relying on a different concept of identity. Those worried about cloning may be concerned with the fact that two individuals are being created genetically identical – *qualitative* identity. In contrast, those objecting to such worries on non-identity grounds claim that cloning is the only possible option for *this* clone to exist – *numerical* identity. We will return to this.

Second case: *wrongful life*. This is the label assigned by tort lawyers to a specific set of cases. Consider a medical practitioner having allegedly harmed a child by misinforming its parents before conception about a specific disability risk. The reassuring misinformation led the parents to decide to conceive a child that unfortunately turned out to be disabled. It is assumed that, had the doctor not misinformed them, this child would not have been conceived. The question is not merely whether such misinformation harmed the parents. The question is whether it also harmed the child. Wrongful life cases force us to locate the exact nature of the problem. Why should the doctor's acts remain immune to criticism? Does it have to do with the lack of direct causal connection between the malpractice and the child's disability, the latter resulting primarily from bad luck in the natural lottery? Or does it rather have to do with the absence of harm, given the non-identity context? We will come back to this too.

Third case: *blind and deaf*. Consider denying blind or deaf parents the right to select blindness or deafness as preferred genetic traits for their future child. Here, two distinct types of concerns about harm are superimposed. One is whether positively selecting deafness or blindness fundamentally differs from selecting other physical traits such as height or hair color or from educating one's child within a certain culture. In other words, the issue is whether selecting such traits can be seen as harmful or wrongful *to the child* once we stop looking at them as disabilities and rather see them as key elements of a merely different identity.[5] A different – and less standard – consideration is whether a harm concept can be used at all here, even if we were all to agree that deafness or blindness are disabilities and do not amount to mere difference. Selecting deafness or blindness before conception entails – given the current state of medicine – that this feature is a necessary condition for this child's very existence. And expressing concern for the child's well-being in order to oppose such a disability selection may require not allowing this very child to come to existence.

These examples show that reproductive choices often fall within the non-identity domain. Yet the problem's scope extends far beyond reproductive choices. To put it differently, many choices happen to be *indirectly* reproductive ones. Timing matters to who gets conceived. And most policies that significantly affect our lives have timing effects. For instance, how we structure the workplace, how we deal with the gendered division of labor, how we organize road networks or the energy policies we implement, all affect the timing of our sexual intercourse through chain effects. And as this gets repeated over generations, the probability that someone be born under two alternative policies of significant impact ends up being minuscule. Environmental policies thus typically fall within the realm of the non-identity problem. This is a challenge to a young climate activist turning to her parents and complaining that they should have acted otherwise. For they may reply, sometimes even in good faith: "Had we acted differently, you would not have existed!"

Harm and non-existence

It is now clear that the problem arises when having certain bodily features or experiencing a certain environment is only avoidable through "one's" non-existence. How does this relate to the ordinary meaning of "harm"? How does "harm" handle cases that involve non-existence as one of the alternative outcomes? How does "harm" handle possibly our most important decisions, i.e. life-and-death ones? If the concept of harm faces difficulties in such cases, it also means that the possibility of characterizing the relevant acts as wrongful is jeopardized, at least if we reject the possibility of harmless wrongdoing.

When invoking a concept of harm, we usually compare the condition of the alleged victim of a contested act with the situation in which this person would (or could) have found herself in the absence of this act. In short, we compare the actual state of this person with her "counterfactual" state.[6] Someone's counterfactual state is the state that should be accessible to that very same person had another course of action taken place. In non-identity cases, it is the very *existence* of the person that is at stake in one of the alternatives.

To understand this, let me move for a minute outside the realm of the non-identity problem. Consider Epicurus' classic discussion on whether killing a person can be said to harm her. Since killing is one of the worst possible actions, having trouble accounting for its harmfulness would be a very significant limitation for our philosophical theories. Yet, if we hold the view that the concept of harm involves comparing two states of the very same person (an actual and a counterfactual one), and that non-existence (the result of the act of killing) cannot be regarded as *the state of a person*, then we may want to conclude that we fall outside the realm of the concept of harm in the killing case.

The idea is *not* that non-existence has a lower value than existence *for this very person*. The point is rather that the ordinary concept of harm is *inapplicable*, because we are simply unable to compare two accessible *states* of the same person.[7] It could follow from this account that killing can be harmless in a significant range of cases, which is of course very troubling.[8] It would also seem to follow that a "pro-life" doctor denying euthanasia to a person in irreversible pain could not be said to harm this person, as the alternative course of action would entail her non-existence. This is also very troubling and hard to swallow.

Let me then move back to child conception – i.e. to the other "end" of our lives – and to non-identity cases. Here, the issue is not whether it is harmful to bring someone from a state of existence to no state at all (rather than a "state" of non-existence). Instead, the issue is whether a given state of a person can be said to be harmful if renouncing the contested action would necessarily – or at least in all likelihood – entail the non-existence of this very person. This remains so regardless of whether we look at this problem *ex post* or *ex ante*. If we stick to the claim that a concept of harm is rendered mute, inapplicable, whenever one of the two possible, alternative "states" of the person at stake is no state at all (i.e. non-existence), then we need to draw the same conclusion in our non-identity case as in the killing case: the "victim" cannot be said to be harmed in a non-identity case by a pre-conception action. This is so whenever the latter is a necessary condition for the person's very existence – at least as long as she has a life worth living, as will be discussed below.

Non-identity, through challenging the applicability of the ordinary concept of harm, questions our sense of moral duty and of justice toward future generations. The problem even touches on issues of legitimacy. Consider John Stuart Mill's "harm" principle. Contrary to what people sometimes assume, it does not amount at all to a general principle of morality – of the type "do not harm others."[9] For, as we will discuss below, there are contexts – such as fair competition – in which we clearly harm others without this necessarily qualifying as wronging them. Instead, the "harm" principle is a principle of political philosophy that merely states a requirement for the legitimacy of state coercion. It does not consider the existence of harm as necessary to justify duties of *justice*. It regards instead the possibility of harm as necessary – and yet not sufficient – to justify the legitimacy of a state restricting the liberties of its citizens. It says that state coercion would be illegitimate if no one were harmed in the absence of such coercion.[10]

If we were to conclude that, due to the non-identity problem, future people cannot be harmed, it follows from Mill's principle that it would be illegitimate for the state to coerce current people – e.g. restrict our right to pollute – in the name of future people. While I will discuss in chapter 5 whether we can coerce future people, we have seen in the introduction that it is at least possible to coerce current citizens in the name of future generations. The issue at stake here is whether coercing citizens can be legitimate if not doing so would be harmless for future people. Hence, the solutions envisaged below are not only relevant to the morality and fairness of procreative and non-procreative policies. They also matter to the legitimacy of future-oriented state coercion. And they potentially challenge Mill's principle.[11]

Harm and distributive justice

As we can see, relying on a standard, comparative-to-counterfactual concept of harm is not straightforward. This is so especially at both ends of life when non-existence is the counterfactual. Given such difficulties, we should gain an understanding of the relationship between harm and justice, especially distributive justice.

When morally concerned about the consequences of our past and current acts for future people, the nature of our worry can be formulated in various ways.[12] Two of them are of special interest to us here. We may object to acts or inactions because they are likely to "*harm* future people." Alternatively, we may blame their authors for being "distributively *unjust* to future people." How do these concepts of "harm" and "justice" relate to one another? This is key in the intergenerational realm because of the connection between the non-identity problem and the concept of harm. In order to clarify the nature of the harm–justice nexus, let me formulate three questions:

Q1: Is the existence of a harm *sufficient* to lead to a duty of justice?
Q2: Is the existence of a harm *necessary* to trigger a duty of justice?
Q3: Does the violation of a duty of justice necessarily amount to a harm?

The first two questions belong to what I refer to as the upward "harm–justice" nexus while the third touches upon the downward "justice–harm" nexus. A negative answer to the first question means that merely claiming that the future has been harmed is *insufficient* to conclude that we should do something about it as a matter of morality or justice.[13] A negative answer to the second question entails that if the non-identity problem prevents us from using the concept of harm in a given context, it does not necessarily render it meaningless to talk about obligations of justice in this very same context. Finally, a negative answer to the third question entails that the idea of harmless wrongdoing could make sense in some specific contexts.

I will address the first two questions here and return to the third one in the next sections. Note as well that there is no one-to-one relationship between answering each of the three questions above and developing each of the three strategies below – i.e. new grammar, containment, and severance. And note that I use "distributive" in a broad sense at this stage, as including principles of justice that care about the distribution or the aggregation of something. I will refine this in the next chapter.

I begin by answering the first question (Q1). If we rely on an ordinary understanding of the concept of harm – to be further explored in the next section – the existence of a harm is *not sufficient* to trigger a moral duty or an obligation of justice to rectify the harm.[14] Not all harms amount to wrongs. Consider the idea of fair competition again. Competitors are constantly inflicting harm on each other. New products and services keep being introduced into markets. They shift clients from one company to another, possibly leading to bankruptcies. Being driven out of business hurts. Yet, if the idea of fair competition makes sense, we should accept that while competitors constantly inflict harm on each other, they are not necessarily acting wrongly.[15] The fair-competition case is meant to illustrate a situation in which not all moves away from a fair baseline require rectification. They may simply move us toward different, yet equally fair, distributive patterns.

Hence, not all harms amount to wrongs. If so, how do we jump from the former to the latter? Concluding that a harm is a wrong requires identifying the breach of a prior duty. Such prior duties can vary in nature.[16] To illustrate, consider two types of harms. One is associated with a violation of a person's bodily integrity: someone cuts your (green) finger. The other involves breaching someone's right to property on external goods: someone destroys your garden. In both cases – "finger" and "garden" – you are being harmed. I will use this example to make two points. First, some prior duties are perceived as stronger than others. I will argue that this explains why rectificatory duties are sometimes perceived as more binding than distributive ones. Second, some prior duties don't seem to obtain in a context of non-overlapping generations. I will argue that this potentially shrinks the range of our intergenerational duties.

For a harm to entail a wrong requires two different paths in our two examples. In the finger case, it rests on the right to bodily integrity, which in turn requires an explanation of why bodily resources should be treated differently from external natural resources.[17] In the garden case, property rights ultimately deserve protection if they reflect a fair distribution of external assets. Why should a harm be compensated if it consists in the victim losing assets that she should not have owned in the first place? Hence, rectificatory claims in this case require a background theory of distributive justice that has to say something about entitlement to external resources.

Yet, if these underlying rights *precede* rectificatory duties, doesn't this clash with the frequent impression that rectificatory duties are *more stringent* than distributive ones? Think about the commonsense intuition that having caused one's neighbor's poverty generates stronger duties toward her than if her poverty resulted from a natural disaster – hereinafter, the "causes of poverty" example. While there may be some truth to this intuition, it is key to understand what drives it. Here is a possible account.

In both cases – "finger" and "garden" – the rectificatory duty is backed by a primary duty. If rectificatory duties are parasitic on these primary duties, they can only derive their stringency from the latter. Hence, the commonsense intuition cannot, strictly speaking, come from a priority of the former over the latter. What is probably at stake instead is that some primary duties are considered as stronger than others. This is the kind of intuition that drives, for instance, the priority assigned by libertarians to self-ownership or the one assigned by Rawlsians to basic liberties. In a nutshell, it is not rectificatory duties that are stronger than distributive ones. It is rather some background duties that are perceived as stronger than others.[18]

Considering the "finger" and "garden" cases, we can assume that people will often regard violations of bodily integrity as worse than violations of the right to property on external resources, or violations of the bodily integrity of humans as worse than the destruction of plants. As a result, a possible account of our "causes of poverty" example is that the action you took to impoverish your neighbor *simultaneously* involved the violation of e.g. her bodily integrity. Similarly, if, in order to destroy your neighbor's garden, you had to cut her finger to prevent her from using a gun to defend herself, the duty of rectification would derive *both* from the violation of her fair property right *and* from the violation of her bodily integrity. This is what could render this duty more stringent than in a natural disaster case. And this strategy is also commonly used in the global justice context to justify our redistributive duties at the transnational level, insisting on the fact that global poverty has been caused to a significant extent by rich countries.[19]

To sum up, as far as the answer to Q1 is concerned, the existence of a harm is insufficient to justify a duty of rectification. In both "finger" and "garden" cases, the duty to rectify also presupposes the violation of a primary right/duty. This is true at least if we are dealing with a standard concept of harm. We will see below that some non-standard notions of harm are such that concluding the existence of a harm *automatically* implies the violation of a *pro tanto* duty of justice. Under such non-standard definitions only, the answer to the first question might have to be affirmative.

I have just proposed an account compatible with the commonsense intuition in the "causes of poverty" case. This brings me to the second point that the finger–garden comparison is meant to illustrate. Here is a conjecture: whenever generations do not overlap, the range of our duties to future generations will be more limited, distributive duties about external goods becoming more central. This is so for reasons that don't reduce to the non-identity problem. They have to do more generally with the relationship between our physical coexistence and the nature of our moral duties. Some duties can only be breached if we physically coexist. Those will be meaningless if we don't coexist. The key point is, then, to find out about the scope of our duties in contexts in which we don't coexist.

For instance, breaching someone's bodily integrity through direct physical aggression is unfeasible without physical coexistence. Hence, part of the "finger" case will not apply beyond the generational overlap. The same may hold for threatening someone's freedom of expression through physically silencing her with a gun threat. Now, once such breaches can be mediated by external objects or procedures that survive our existence, the related duties could be breached without the need for physical coexistence. Leaving a chemical or a virus in the environment may threaten future people's bodily integrity.[20] Transmitting a non-democratic society may threaten future people's freedom of expression beyond our death. In addition, "garden" and "finger" don't capture the whole range of our potential duties. For instance, relational duties of respect may hold beyond the overlap too. I cannot go into details at this stage about which of our duties would survive the absence of overlap. I am merely conjecturing that their range is likely to be narrower and that, as a result, the relative space occupied by distributive duties about external objects, be they material or immaterial, will become more central. Note as well that our climate explorations in chapter 4 will provide still another perspective on this.

At this stage, it has become clear that an account of intergenerational justice needs to weave its way through several constraints when it comes to non-overlapping generations. First, the non-identity problem challenges the use of some form of harm-based concern to justify duties to the future. Second, some duties, as far as they require that people coexist, do not obtain toward the future. Third, once duties are breached, room for rectification is also more limited, those having violated such duties to the future being dead by the time the victims of such violations will suffer their effects. The conjunction of these three constraints places us on a first type of narrow path – we will point to another type of narrow path in chapter 2. To sum up, when generations don't overlap, our repertoire of justice is restricted because of the difficulties we face in using the concept of harm, the out-of-scopeness of some non-distributive duties, and the impossibility of activating rectificatory duties in time once violations have occurred.

We can now return to our three questions. Let me move to the second one (Q2). It focuses on necessity rather than sufficiency. My claim is that the existence of a prior harm is *not necessary* to trigger duties. Owing something to someone out of a distributive justice obligation does not presuppose that I harmed that person in the first place. Our "causes of poverty" example illustrates this. Progressive taxation can be justified even if the poverty of the least well-off cannot be causally traced to the behaviors of the wealthier. We may owe others redistribution simply because it would be unjust to let them face alone the consequences of their brute bad luck.

Hence, what matters at this stage is that we can *sever* the *upward* harm–justice nexus: the existence of a harm is neither sufficient nor necessary for duties of justice to obtain. As a result, if the possibility of *harming* future people is jeopardized by the non-identity problem, it does not necessarily follow that this would prevent us from having duties of justice toward future people. This is what we will find out through looking at three strategies that I will now introduce.

First, we can try and come up with alternative concepts of harm – call this *"new grammar."* It implies that it matters to a theory of justice to preserve, as far as possible, some articulation between harm and justice. It may go as far as exploring the possibility of equating the absence of harm with meeting the demands of a full theory of justice.

Second, we can try and show that even if we stick to the ordinary concept of harm, there are ways of defending significant obligations of intergenerational justice. Here, the idea is to show that the non-identity challenge is not as "lethal" as one may think – call it *"containment."* It neither questions the connection between harm and justice, nor renounces a standard concept of harm. Instead, it insists on generational overlap. Note that the notion of containment entails that, in the other cases that remain *within* the containment zone, we simply might have to bite the bullet and modify our moral intuitions.

Third, we can try and sever more widely our obligations of justice from the difficulties associated with the harm concept – call it *"severance."* It explores the extent to which we can insulate duties of justice from contagion by the non-identity problem through severing justice from harm. The basic intuition is the following. The non-identity problem threatens our ability to rely on a concept of harm in specific settings. Showing that the link between justice and harm is looser than we anticipated should allow us to conclude that our obligations of *justice* are less vulnerable to the non-identity problem than we thought.

I will examine these three avenues in turn. As they unfold, the reader will note that each of them involves its own way of understanding the relationship between harm and justice. I will also try and preserve as much as possible the sense that if a course of action is bad or worse than another, it needs to be bad or worse *for someone*. We will see, however, that "severance" will have more trouble sticking to this "person-affecting" line of thought. Also, the three strategies should be read as potentially complementary rather than mutually exclusive, because their scope may not fully coincide. Different concepts of harm could have partly overlapping scopes. And I don't assume here that the difficulties encountered in non-identity contexts, as well as in other contexts, necessarily call for abandoning the ordinary concept of harm altogether over its whole range.

Strategy 1: new grammar

Let me envisage here two alternatives to the ordinary concept of harm. The latter compares the current condition of a person with a counterfactual condition of that same person. One alternative concept compares the current condition of a person (or group) with the counterfactual condition of *another* person (or group) who is subjected to the action under the alternative course of action, regardless of whether it is the same person (or group). For instance, in a wrongful life case, had the medical doctor offered the right diagnosis about the very serious health risks associated with Begonia's parent's genetic condition, the latter would have gone for medically assisted reproduction and given birth to Paloma instead. Paloma would have enjoyed a much better physical condition. Under this first alternative concept of harm, while Begonia's life is worth living, she could claim to have been harmed because Paloma would have been even better off than her.

Of course, this identity-independent alternative would be moot had Begonia's parents decided not to have any child at all. However, something else is more worrying. While we should remain open to the possibility of a non-person-affecting account of our obligations of *justice*

– to which I return below – the concept of *harm* itself should preserve some degree of person-affectingness, the idea being that I am harming *this* person. It could possibly make sense to claim – axiologically – that the world would have been a better one had Paloma been born rather than Begonia. It might even make sense under certain conditions to claim – morally – that the parents would have had a moral duty to bring Paloma into existence rather than Begonia, had they known about the risk and had they had the possibility of avoiding it at little cost to themselves. Yet claiming that Begonia was *harmed* because Paloma could have been born instead does not sufficiently preserve the initial meaning of harm. It entails that it is bad *for a person* to be brought into existence if *someone else* with a better condition could have been brought into existence *instead*. My view is that such a concept of harm overstretches things. My main concern here is meaninglessness.[21]

Consider now another alternative concept of harm. It does not call for a comparison between Begonia's actual and hypothetical condition. Nor does it call for a comparison between Begonia's actual condition and Paloma's hypothetical condition. Instead, it requires a comparison between Begonia's actual condition and an external standard, for instance a minimum threshold of well-being defined a priori. Under this concept, a person is harmed by an action or abstention, including one that could be a necessary condition for her very existence, if her life can be said to be bad for her *in absolute terms*. This is often framed as a life falling below the threshold of a life worth living. This threshold-based concept is meaningful, contrary to the "comparative-to-others" one. It says that a life can be bad *for its bearer*, despite being the *only possible* life for *this* person. And it claims that knowingly bringing such a person into existence can be harmful.

Is this comparative-to-norm concept different from the ordinary concept? Yes. To understand it, let us describe a "harm" situation as a move from one state of the world – the initial/counterfactual state – to another – the end/

actual state – a move that entails a loss for at least one person: the harmed person. In our discussion about Q1, we stressed that under an ordinary concept of harm, an implicit normative assumption obtains about the fairness of the *initial/counterfactual* state. In a sense, we can thus say that the ordinary concept of harm is implicitly normative. This is so if we accept the view that we would not tend to characterize as a "harm" the fact of depriving someone – albeit after due process – of something that she was not legitimately entitled to in the first place.

Yet, while the ordinary concept of harm points to a departure from a fair initial state that entails a loss for one person, it does not automatically tell us whether the end state is morally problematic or unfair. This is what the fair-competition example revealed. Someone can be said to have been harmed even if both the initial state and the end state remain morally unproblematic. While the fairness of the initial state appears to be a necessary condition for the existence of a harm, the existence of this harm is not a sufficient condition for the unfairness of the end state. Now, like the ordinary concept, the *comparative-to-norm* concept of harm sets a norm. However, unlike for the ordinary concept, this norm applies to the *end/actual state* rather than relying on a comparison with the initial state. It claims, for instance, that an act that brings a person into existence harms this person if she *ends up* being born with a life not worth living.

To fully understand the new grammar associated with the comparative-to-norm concept of harm, let me clarify how the comparative-to-norm concept handles the harm–wrong gap. The standard concept of harm, while implying the fairness of the initial/counterfactual state, remains agnostic about the fairness of the end/actual state. In contrast, isn't it the case that the comparative-to-norm concept of harm, since it focuses on the fairness of the end/actual state, completely closes the gap between harm and wrong? The existence of a harm would suffice to conclude the existence of a wrong, as if the violation of a right were to automatically imply the violation of a correlative duty. The fair-competition case indicates that this does not need to be so under the ordinary concept of harm. I am inclined to think that whether relying on a threshold concept of harm closes the harm–wrong gap depends on whether the threshold provides us with *pro tanto* (intermediary) or all-things-considered (final) reasons to act or abstain. Whenever the threshold-based standard of harm is a *pro tanto* one, it remains possible that while the person is harmed, she isn't automatically wronged, other considerations having to be assessed to bridge the gap. In contrast, where the threshold-based standard of harm is an *all-things-considered* one, being harmed would *automatically* entail being wronged.[22]

We then need to look at threshold candidates to assess whether they should be considered as *pro tanto* standards. If we rely on a specific right as a standard of harm (e.g. the right to non-discrimination or to a clean environment), and accept the view that some rights can be violated in the name of satisfying other rights, then the mere violation of a right does not tell us automatically whether the right-bearer has been wronged.[23] If we rely instead on a "life-not-worth-living" threshold as a standard of harm, whenever the person finds herself avoidably below the threshold, she is wronged, as society has a duty to make sure it is avoided, unless the person herself objects. I would tend to consider, then, that the person remaining under such a threshold is being both harmed and wronged. This could entail – under specific circumstances – a duty not to bring such persons into existence or to assist them in committing suicide. Finally, were we to rely on a complete theory of justice as a standard of harm, the harm–wrong gap would also be bridged, as we clearly face an all-things-considered standard. This is relevant to our approach to Q3 above.

At this stage, we see that both the ordinary and the comparative-to-norm concepts of harm involve something normative. It is implicit in the former case and explicit in the latter. However, while the norm applies to the *initial/counterfactual* state under the ordinary concept, it applies to the *end/actual* state under the alternative concept of harm. Also, while the ordinary concept requires a comparison between the two states (the initial and the end one), the alternative concept does not require such a comparison. And this explains its robustness in non-identity contexts in which there is no initial or counterfactual state. Finally, while the standard concept of harm preserves the harm–wrong gap, this is not necessarily so for the comparative-to-norm concept. Closing the harm–wrong gap is a feature of the alternative concept. It is not as such a problem, as we don't stretch the concept of harm to the point where it would become meaningless to say "this person has been harmed." It merely draws our attention to the fact that we are operating under an alternative grammar. While a sufficientarian theory of justice can still be severed from the ordinary concept of harm in line with our earlier discussion of the upward harm–justice nexus, it would be squeezed inside the comparative-to-norm standard of harm, and become consubstantial to it, if no further demands of justice were to obtain once the sufficiency threshold has been reached.

New grammar's limitations

There are limitations associated with relying on a "comparative-to-norm" concept to overcome the non-identity challenge. Let me stress two of them. The nature of such limitations differs, depending on whether we rely on a narrow, incomplete standard or rather on a fuller theory of justice to assess harm.

Consider first a *narrow* interpretation of the comparative-to-norm standard, one under which harm occurs whenever the person finds herself below, say, a "life-not-worth-living" standard. There is a sense in which the life-worth-living, threshold-based concept of harm allows us a more complete approach than the comparative-to-counterfactual ordinary concept. It can conclude that a harm exists even when there would have been no other child in the alternative. However, the life-worth-living threshold concept remains incomplete: there is a significant number of non-identity cases where we may want to claim that an action or abstention was morally objectionable notwithstanding the fact that the person's life resulting from this action or abstention remains clearly worth living.

To illustrate, in an energy policy case, we can have an energy choice that has deleterious health effects on our children with no significant benefits to us, and that affects who ends up being born. However, if this problematic choice does not render the life of our children not worth living, it won't be more objectionable under this threshold concept of harm than under the standard concept of harm. This holds for cloning decisions, for most wrongful life cases or ages of reproduction deemed non-optimal, and more generally for a wide range of non-reproductive choices, as long as the life of those born as a result is overall worth living.[24] This is a serious limitation. We should not wait until we go as far as rendering the Earth uninhabitable and until our lives become wretched before concluding that our (in)action toward the future is unfair or morally problematic. We may want to object to a significant range of behaviors *even if* they are not as deleterious as rendering our lives not worth living.[25]

As a response, we could go for a more demanding, *broader* threshold-based standard. It would express, through the lens of a harm concept, a fuller set of rights or a larger segment of a theory of justice. It could say that people are harmed if their rights are violated or if they find themselves below a sufficiency threshold, e.g. one that requires each of us to have her basic needs provided for. The nature of this move is quite specific. It begins with the assumption that we want to keep using a concept of harm in a non-identity context. It transforms the meaning of this concept of harm. And it gives substance to it through squeezing part of a theory of justice into it. Because we are not talking anymore about merely *pro tanto* considerations, such a broad threshold-based concept entails that we end up with a concept of harm that is also a concept of wrong.

There is a significant limitation to this "squeezing-in" strategy. It only works with theories that contain a threshold-based component and where it plays a central role. Many of them include such a threshold. This is the case of views that incorporate a sufficientarian component, be they of egalitarian or utilitarian pedigree. And it is also the case of some right-based views. But it is definitely not the case for more *continuous* egalitarian, prioritarian, or utilitarian views. For instance, a theory that claims that a distribution of resources is fairer if the least well-off is better off under it than the least well-off under the alternative policy requires a comparison with possibly someone else in a counterfactual. And this bring us back to the meaning problems encountered in the case of a comparative-to-others concept of harm. In short, anyone holding a general conception of justice that is not (exclusively) sufficientarian will not be able to overcome the non-identity problem through merely shifting to a comparative-to-norm concept of harm and squeezing in the theory of justice she champions. This is an important reason to seek alternative solutions that don't pass through the prism of an alternative concept of harm, be it a comparative-to-others or a comparative-to-norm one.

Strategy 2: containment and deathbed assessment

Consider, then, a second strategy to deal with the difficulties experienced by the comparative-to-counterfactual concept of harm in non-identity cases. While this strategy is both significant and revealing, impatient readers may move straight to the third – and main – strategy if they wish. The second strategy neither relies on modifying the concept of harm, nor entails conflating the demands of justice with the possible scope of harm in non-identity cases. Instead, it *insulates* some of the demands of justice from the difficulties encountered in non-identity cases. It does so by insisting on what is still possible and required *after* the child's conception in non-identity cases. I refer to this strategy as "containment."

Consider Nasreddin and his daughter Fatma, two representative members of two successive and overlapping generations. Nasreddin's generation owes Fatma's ten units of "stuff" per capita, as a matter of distributive justice between birth cohorts. This "stuff" includes goods and services, understood broadly. Whether Nasreddin has fulfilled his intergenerational duties toward Fatma ought to be assessed *by the end of his life*. Now, imagine that Nasreddin's pre-conception policy choices and actions happen to destroy five units of the stuff that could have been passed on to Fatma. While such destruction was easily avoidable, Nasreddin simply didn't care. Because of non-identity, this destruction of five units before Fatma's conception cannot as such be said to harm her – in the standard sense. Does it follow that Nasreddin merely ought to transfer five units – rather than ten – to fulfil his lifelong intergenerational obligations?

The containment strategy answers in the negative. Given the overlap between Nasreddin's and Fatma's lives, it is still *possible* for Nasreddin's generation to work toward transferring the right amount of goods and services *after* Fatma's conception. In addition, while the timing of some intergenerational transfers over one's lifetime matters, for others it is less important. Delaying baby care or anticipating inheritance makes a difference. Yet, for a large segment of our duties between birth cohorts, what matters is what will have been transferred overall *by the end of a generation's life*, leading to what I will refer to as "deathbed assessment." The timing of intergenerational transfers is less crucial for birth cohorts than for age groups. This is so partly because transfers to the next generation are not meant to be consumed merely by the next generation. As a result, Nasreddin can still "catch up" after Fatma's conception to avoid not fulfilling his "entire-life" intergenerational obligations. It potentially leaves his entire-life duties unaffected. Hence, we can contain the impact of non-identity on pre-conception duties, and as a result, potentially immunize our entire-life duties from the impact of the non-identity problem.

Besides the stress on the overlap, two ideas are central for the containment strategy. The first one is that the duties of a generation toward the next should be assessed on *aggregate*, by the end of a generation's life – what I call "deathbed assessment." This echoes to some degree the complete-life idea on the entitlements side discussed in the introduction. Also, aggregate duties should not be sensitive to whether acts taking place before the conception of the second generation are themselves immune to moral criticism due to the non-identity problem. By "aggregate," I mean something that is assessed neither on a periodical basis, nor at a single moment before the duty-holder's death.[26] Moreover, renouncing the aggregate approach would unnecessarily restrict duty-holders' freedom to decide among two equally effective paths to transfer resources to the next generation, each of them having a different time structure. This is why the pre-conception destruction of five units of "stuff" in our example will leave unaffected the ten-units duty of Nasreddin toward Fatma. Whether Nasreddin rendered his job more difficult in the end should not be taken into account here, regardless of whether his earlier destructive acts were technically harmless or not.

The second idea draws on the distinction between negative and positive duties. Imagine that our intergenerational duties were exclusively *negative – i.e. duties to abstain*. The violation of his negative duty by Nasreddin before Fatma's conception would be immune from moral criticism, under the standard concept of harm. As to Nasreddin's duties after Fatma's conception, they would be limited to negative ones too. If we were to stick to negative duties, there is no way our containment strategy could require that more than the five units of stuff left be transferred to Fatma.

However, intergenerational duties ought to include *positive* ones too. One reason is that, as discussed in the introduction, while our duties as a cohort exceed those that we have as an age group, the former also *include* the latter. And care duties between age groups typically involve *positive* duties. The difficulty is that care duties may not suffice for our containment strategy, as they only represent a limited part of what we owe the next generation and as timing is central for them. Yet there are further reasons to include positive duties in our duties between birth cohorts. For instance, when we consume non-renewable natural resources, several views require compensating such losses in resource availability with extra technology (substitution). Such technology needs to be invented, developed, and taught through patient work. Hence, if we cannot live purely on renewable resources, intergenerational obligations cannot remain purely negative, since some substitution will be needed. This illustrates another reason why intergenerational duties ought to include positive duties, this time of a type for which the timing of duty fulfillment is less crucial. And if our intergenerational duties are not strictly negative, "containment" can work.

In short, the containment strategy works if our duties to the next generation are not strictly negative and if their fulfillment is assessed in a full life-cycle way, as a package. It accepts the harmlessness of pre-conception violations of duties. It stresses that duties of intergenerational justice survive the conception of the next generation. And it can even claim that the violation of such package duties of justice would indeed be *harmful* to the next generation. This last step points to a different way in which harm and justice can be linked. It allows us to address the worry implied in Q3 above: "can duties of justice make sense if their violation is harmless?" Under the containment strategy, their violation is *not* harmless, despite the harmlessness of pre-conception destructions.

Nasreddin's duties survive his child's conception and to that extent they are not subject to the non-identity challenge. To be clear, there is of course a wide range of duties that we should continuously comply with. For instance, it is obvious that Nasreddin's actions before Fatma's conception would provide him with no good reason to violate her bodily integrity or freedom of expression at later points in her life. What the idea of deathbed assessment strategy adds is that even for duties that are not continuous, such as what we owe the next generation in terms of external resources on distributive grounds, there is room for escaping the consequences of the non-identity problem after conception, without even renouncing the standard concept of harm.

Containment's limitations

The containment strategy allows us to defend duties of intergenerational justice within the overlap. This is significant. If Nasreddin and Fatma each have a life expectancy of eighty years and if Nasreddin becomes her father at the age of thirty, Nasreddin's duties of inter-generational justice get insulated from the non-identity objection for more than eighty years.[27] This is enough to deal with some long-term issues, even without stretching the non-identity-free zone further through invoking the sequentiality of intergenerational chains. Beyond the strict overlap period of fifty years itself, the containment strategy extends before Fatma's birth and beyond Nasreddin's death. If Nasreddin knowingly committed "harmless" destruction before Fatma's conception, these will *not* reduce his distributive obligations accordingly. And if some of Nasreddin's actions that took place during the overlap period will predictably affect Fatma after Nasreddin's death, they will also not be subject to the non-identity exemption. He will be constrained in his actions during the overlap even if their effects on Fatma are only expected to take place after his death. Hence, when we refer to the overlap here, we include some consequences of actions that take place both before Fatma's existence and after Nasreddin's existence.

And yet, as broad as it may be, the containment strategy is limited in two important ways. The first limitation concerns the bioethics issues subject to the non-identity challenge that we discussed earlier: cloning, optimal age of reproduction, wrongful life, ... Those ethically concerned with such cases want to avoid the very act of cloning itself, the very medical misinformation leading to the conception of a disabled child, or the very fact of having a too large or too small age gap between biological parents and their children. The consequences of these acts are *irreversible*. Of course, the general distributive obligations that parents and society at large have to their children may have to be adjusted if we consider that the condition of these children is disadvantageous. Also, the division of labor between parents and society may have to be adjusted if parents choose to go for some procreative strategies that impose unjustifiable costs on others. However, if we stick to the standard concept of harm, the very fact of selecting a child because of her deafness or as a clone, or the very fact of deciding to have a child at the age of sixty, cannot be objected to, at least not out of concern for the interest of the child. The containment strategy cannot prevent such a conclusion. We may have to bite the bullet in these cases: no harm to the child – which leaves open the possibility of harm to others and of duties of justice to the child and to others.

The second limitation of the containment strategy is potentially more serious. The strategy rests on the fact that it is possible to fulfil one's distributive duties during the overlap period and that such duties would then not be subject to the non-identity problem. However, for generations that never overlap, that are remote from each other, all the actions or inactions of the early generation will fall before the conception of the late generation, and will therefore be subject to the non-identity problem. What avenues, then, remain open if we want to object to the behavior of earlier generations in *non-overlap* contexts that are subject to the non-identity problem?

Beyond the overlap, we can of course rely on the threshold-based, comparative-to-norm concept of harm, with its limitations. Yet there are at least two further possibilities. One consists in going radically for the severance approach. I will discuss it in the next section. The other consists in endorsing an indirect account of our duties toward remote generations, understood as duties toward intermediary generations that overlap with us and that would, in turn, have obligations toward other generations that overlap with them while not with us. The existence of a sequence or chain of overlaps is essential in this respect.[28] The strategy amounts to relying on the idea that what is unacceptable in taking action that has adverse effects on non-overlapping remote generations is that it is going to render compliance with their distributive obligations harder for the intermediary duty-holding generation with which we and they overlap. This is a promising strategy. It may even allow us to address "time-bomb" cases, i.e. cases of actions that have an impact on non-overlapping future generations without having any impact on intermediary generations with which we overlap. Time bombs can be addressed through the indirect strategy because they may entail increased duties on the part of intermediary generations toward their successors, even if intermediary generations are not themselves impacted by the time bombs. We will see, however, at the end of chapter 3 and in chapter 4 that this indirect strategy has limitations too.

Strategy 3: full severance

So far, I have explored the possibility of departing from the ordinary concept of harm through relying on a comparative-to-norm concept of harm. I have also presented the containment strategy, which remains within the ambit of the ordinary concept of harm. And I have mentioned the indirect strategy, which relies on the succession of duties of overlapping generations toward one another to keep non-overlapping generations within our moral reach. I will now explore one last avenue. It consists in pushing the disconnection between harm and injustice further. At the beginning of this chapter, I stressed that the concept of harm was neither sufficient nor even necessary to trigger duties of justice. While I have touched upon Q3 here and there, it is now time to come back to it more directly.

The comparative-to-norm concept of harm implies a very specific relationship between harm and justice. In presenting the containment strategy, I also insisted on the fact that it is compatible with relying on the ordinary concept of harm. In that sense, the containment approach does not force us to renounce the view that the violation of our life-cycle duties toward the next generation can be seen as harmful in the standard sense. The same holds for the indirect strategy, which expresses concerns for the impact of our acts on the ability of the next generation to fulfil its duties toward its successors.

What I want to ask here is whether it really matters to be able to claim that the violation of a duty necessarily implies that we *harm* the beneficiary of this duty. If it didn't matter, we could then open the avenue to cases of harmless wrongdoing. We could address issues of justice between generations without the need to rely on the concept of harm. Upstream, duties of justice would occur even if no prior harm took place. And downstream, duties of justice would remain even if their violation could not be characterized as harmful. What the severance of the upstream "harm–justice" nexus invites us to do is to question the need for a downstream "justice–harm" nexus. Full severance would entail that we endorse what has been referred to as a "non-person-affecting" view. We have tried so far to stay away from it and we have shown that there is room for important alternatives in this respect. However, it is important to face it as a real possibility as well.

For instance, if we are an egalitarian, we don't want members of the next generation to be less well-off than we are for the mere reason that they happen to come into existence at another time than us. How important is it, in the end, that we claim that violating the duty of equality will be harmful to them rather than "merely" unjust, especially if we accept the parasitic nature of harm and rectification on (distributive) justice? Is it the case that our moral standards are likely to go wild as soon as we accept breaking not only the upstream "harm–justice" nexus but also the downstream "justice–harm" nexus? We will still care about justice because we care about people, whoever they are. And we will still be able to provide an account of justice based, among other things, on an impartiality assumption.

The severance of the upstream "harm–justice" nexus suggests that the reason why we express concern for justice does not need to be framed as a concern for harm in the first place. All this invites us to envisage the relationship between justice and harm as looser than it may seem. And it suggests that non-person-affecting approaches might end up being less mysterious than they may seem at first sight. If we accept this, we open the gates to freeing justice from the non-identity problem, and to a full scope of intergenerational justice beyond the overlap, without the need for indirect approaches. In other words, we make it possible to defend obligations of justice *toward* future generations all the way down, and not merely *about* future generations whenever they don't overlap with us.[29] This is, I think, the way to go. It is meaningful, robust, and straightforward.

Conclusion

Let me wrap up. I have explored how the non-identity challenge can be taken seriously while keeping in mind the need to properly articulate harm and justice. I have looked at the nature and scope of the non-identity problem and the extent to which it threatens our ability to rely on an ordinary concept of harm in non-identity contexts. I explored the possibility of alternative concepts of harm, concluding that while comparative-to-norm concepts are a meaningful option, their practical implications are limited in two ways. I also insisted in this context on the nature of the relationship of justice and harm that the alternative concept implies. I then presented the containment strategy. While relying on an ordinary concept of harm and remaining within the ambit of person-affecting intuitions, it allows us to broaden the scope of non-identity-immune duties of justice. It takes into consideration both the importance of generational overlap and the partly positive nature of our intergenerational duties. I also mentioned very briefly what I called the indirect strategy. I concluded with the suggestion that even if the new grammar and containment strategies already allow us to justify a significant number of intergenerational duties, we should not close the door to the possibility of duties of justice toward non-overlapping generations the violation of which would not imply any harm in the standard sense. The possibility of acting unjustly without acting harmfully is all the easier to contemplate if we look carefully at the nature of the connection between justice and harm at the upstream end.[30]

At this stage, I have been more concerned about defending the very possibility of obligations of justice to the future. Still, in the course of our discussion, I have already had a chance to allude to some of the distinctions that are relevant to the content of those duties, such as those between threshold-based and non-threshold-based views, or between negative and positive duties. I will now turn more closely to the content of such intergenerational duties.

2

How much do we owe the future?

In the previous chapter, I addressed the non-identity challenge. It potentially exempts us from a very significant range of duties to the future, duties that commonsense morality would otherwise tend to endorse. I proposed three strategies aimed at preserving significant duties to the future. In so doing, I stressed that the role of the concept of harm in a theory of justice is more limited than some readers may have thought. In the present chapter, I move to a positive account of the content of our duties to other generations. In a sense, the non-identity challenge was so radical that it questioned *whether* we had any duties to the future *at all*. The present chapter will contribute toward telling us *what* duties of justice we have to the future.

I proceed in three steps. First, I present four accounts of justice toward the next generation(s), framing them within a language of "generational savings" and "generational dis-savings."[1] Second, I discuss whether an alternative framing is possible, one that would not give such a central role to the notions of savings and dis-savings. Third, I focus on understanding the relationship between inter-generational justice and sustainability. Moving through these three sections will involve gradually putting our initial framing into perspective.

Also, throughout the chapter, I will bridge conceptual steps about how to frame our duties and their nature with normative claims about which accounts should be rejected or endorsed. Conceptual work is central for normative exploration. It may question the meaningfulness or distinctiveness of some of the normative proposals. It may also open new alternatives that would be normatively more adequate. Again, I fully understand that some readers may be concerned about avoiding philosophical hairsplitting in times of climate collapse and dire poverty. Yet seemingly minute theoretical differences may lead to huge ones at the policy level. The view that citizens end up endorsing on intergenerational duties matters. And it may make a practical difference at both the collective and individual levels.

Intergenerational justice: four accounts

Generational (dis-)savings

Here is a simplified framework. I will focus on *how much* "stuff" each generation should transfer to the next one(s). I will return to what this "stuff" should be in the next chapter. Here, I focus exclusively on its *size*. At this stage, we just need to understand it broadly as including natural resources, but also "technology," broadly understood, ranging from cooking recipes to surgery procedures, engineering techniques, social and political institutions, languages, world visions, or ways of life. For those familiar with the grammar of theories of justice, the present chapter focuses on the principle (or pattern) of intergenerational justice whereas the next chapter focuses on its metrics (or currency). The purpose of this simplifying framework is to reveal *qualitatively* distinct approaches to intergenerational justice.

I will rely on the notions of savings and dis-savings. Generational *savings* obtain whenever a generation as a whole transfers to the next one *more* than it inherited from the previous one. The word "savings" typically carries not only a conservation meaning ("keep this for tomorrow!") but also an "aggradation" one ("invest this to get more tomorrow!"). Generational savings go beyond mere preservation. In contrast, generational *dis-savings* mean that a generation transfers to the next one *less* than it inherited from the previous one. Hence, we face three options, "dis-savings" and its two opposites: transferring strictly as much ("preservation") or more ("savings"). The "savings/dis-savings" distinction combines with three modalities. We can either authorize, impose, or prohibit generational dis-savings or savings. Each of the four views presented below, then, consists in a combination of principles, each of them mixing respectively savings, dis-savings, or preservation with authorization, obligation, or prohibition. I will match each combination with an underlying theory of justice.

View 1: non-decline
The first view – hereinafter referred to as "non-decline" – prohibits generational dis-savings while authorizing generational savings. We should not transfer less to the next generation than we inherited. Yet we are allowed to transfer more if we so wish, as a generation. I take this view to be very common. It is also central to the sustainability debate. I leave aside for the next chapter important issues, such as whether *prohibiting dis-savings* – a feature common to three of the views I will present – is compatible with consuming non-renewable resources. Here, I concentrate on linking "non-decline" with a "reciprocity-based" approach to justice, on finding whether and why the latter may ground the former.[2]

At its core, a reciprocity view about justice requires that if I benefit from x units of "stuff," I should make sure to return the equivalent at some point. On reflection, a reciprocity view is unlikely to fit with the general intuitions about justice that many of us endorse, which contrasts with the first impression that most of us may defend the "non-decline" view. What is unattractive about reciprocity is that it typically equates justice with the *absence of net transfers*: I should return to others roughly as much as what I benefited from, regardless of my abilities.[3] If you think that the most disadvantaged – for instance the quadriplegics among us – should be net beneficiaries of at least some redistributive transfers, the reciprocity view, given its "no net transfer" core, cannot serve as a general account of justice. This matters when considering whether to endorse it as an underlying justification for an intergenerational principle.

Leaving this aside for a moment, it is the conjunction of two features that happens to render a reciprocity view both attractive and conducive to non-decline in an intergenerational context. One feature is the plasticity of the reciprocity concept. The other is the nature of intergenerational relations. I look at each of them in turn.

First, the concept's plasticity allows us to specify it further in two steps. Step 1: we can move from direct to *indirect* reciprocity. Direct reciprocity refers to a requirement to reciprocate to the *same* person (or group). In an intergenerational context, *direct* reciprocity means, for instance, that we owe elderly care to our parents because we benefited from child care *from them*. An indirect version disconnects the identity of the "initial" benefit-provider from that of the "final" benefit-recipient. The duty-holder is then "caught" in between. This is so when one says: "Because I received *x* from the previous generation, I owe *x* to the next generation." Here, I leave aside a series of issues about direct intergenerational reciprocity. For instance, what follows for direct-reciprocity advocates if our societies turn out to be pro-child, namely if transfers to the elderly tend to be systematically smaller than transfers to children?

Step 2: in an intergenerational context, once we turn to indirect reciprocity, we can also decide to focus on only one of its two directions along the time axis, which is not possible with direct reciprocity. More specifically, we can focus on *descending* indirect reciprocity, on forward transfers, as in "I owe *x* to the next generation because the previous generation did *x* for me (or because the next generation will do *x* for its successors)." In contrast, ascending, backward transfers obtain, for example, in a retirement pension model claiming that "I owe a pension to my parents because they did the same for their parents (or because our children will do the same for us)."

Having shifted to *indirect descending* reciprocity, we can then come to the *second* feature that allows us to match "non-decline" and "reciprocity." Why does the prohibition on net transfers at the heart of reciprocity not translate into a *prohibition* on generational *savings*? Because *the future is open*, indefinitely – which, admittedly, does not mean "infinitely." This contrasts with transfers between neighbors operating in a closed circle or in a "closed" society of contemporaries. Imagine that one generation inherited five units of "stuff" from the previous one. The non-decline view requires that it returns no less than five units to the next generation. If it wanted to return six units instead and if generations were neighbors in a closed circle (or if the number of generations were finite), a reciprocity view should also prohibit generational savings.[4] Otherwise, some of us would end up being forced into the position of net beneficiaries, having received more than they would have reciprocated.

In contrast, in an intergenerational setting with an indefinite horizon, transferring six units to the next generation does not necessarily transform the next generation into a net beneficiary. For the latter can make sure that it transfers in turn at least six units to its followers, and so on and so forth, indefinitely. Hence, it is the openness to the future of *descending* intergenerational relations that enables reciprocity to *allow us* to give "back" to the future more than we received from the past, without forcing anyone to have received more than she will end up having given back.

This is also one of the reasons why endorsing a backward-oriented, *ascending* indirect-reciprocity logic as a general model may be problematic. Think about "I owe my parents as much as they transferred to their parents" or "I owe my parents as much as my children will (or should) transfer to me." Under a reciprocity view, what I transfer to my parents should be neither larger or nor smaller than what they transferred to their parents or what our children will transfer to us. This closes the door to the ascending equivalent of authorizing savings, namely authorizing our children to return *more* to us than we transferred to our own parents. In addition, the need to get the scheme started entails the unavoidable violation of this rule through the existence of an initial "free lunch" generation, especially visible in pay-as-you-go pension schemes. Such an original "sin" has no equivalent in the descending, forward indirect-reciprocity case.

In a nutshell, "non-decline" is a view that many may consider endorsing. Reciprocity can be understood as "indirect" and "descending." And the latter, in an open-future context, supports a "non-decline" rule of thumb. Yet reciprocity as a general account of justice is unlikely to be attractive on reflection, due to its rejection of net, non-reciprocated transfers. This invites us to consider alternatives.

View 2: better future
The second view shares the idea that generational dis-savings should be prohibited. Yet instead of merely authorizing generational savings, it renders them compulsory. For this view, it is unjust *not* to transfer more to the next generation than we inherited from the previous one. The intuition may derive some of its initial appeal from the view that parents often hold, at the family level, when they sacrifice themselves to ensure that their children will experience a better life than theirs. Yet, on reflection, it is not straightforward to justify this as a duty, be it at the parental level or at the generational level. I will show how a utilitarian account of justice can support this view.[5] I will insist on two features of intergenerational relations – different from the "openness to the future" one – that are central in leading utilitarians to support "better future."

Let me first say a few words about utilitarianism. It is a view about morality and justice with two core components. On the one hand, its principle is *aggregative* – as opposed to distributive. It commands that we maximize the *total* amount of an *x* in society, even if doing so were to require a very unequal distribution of this *x*. On the other hand, its metrics, i.e. this *x* to be maximized, is *welfarist*. Welfare can be defined as the satisfaction of people's own preferences. It means that utilitarians can take seriously what people consider to be good for themselves.

Too often we reject utilitarianism for the wrong reasons. Many non-utilitarians still give some weight to efficiency in their account of justice. This is the case, for example, for leximin egalitarians – see below – that value efficiency-based departures from equality provided that such gains are needed to improve the situation of the least well-off. Also, many non-utilitarians incorporate some welfarist element in their metrics. This is the case, for instance, for egalitarians that claim that we should equalize "opportunity for welfare." This stresses the need for a precise diagnosis of *what* may go wrong with utilitarianism.

In the generational realm, a utilitarian policy maker aims at maximizing the size of the intergenerational "pie" of welfare (or well-being). As an aggregativist, she looks impartially at all the generations and identifies the path that best maximizes the *total* amount of well-being across these generations, including both current and future ones. It aims at maximizing such cross-generational well-being even if it means that some generations will experience less well-being than others, or even if some of them are "sacrificed" for the whole's sake.

In an *intra*generational setting, there could be various reasons to sacrifice the well-being of some for the sake of maximizing the total amount of well-being. This may include division-of-labor reasons leading to efficiency gains, as when we send some soldiers to the front line rather than sending all of us. Incentive-based reasons also get invoked to justify inequalities in the name of efficiency.

This is so whenever a fiscal policy departs from equalizing net wages in the name of maximizing total well-being, out of concern for the disincentive effects of taxation on the most productive and out of respect for a norm prohibiting forced labor. This also suggests the possibility of sacrificing some *generations* in the name of maximizing total cross-generational well-being. In fact, utilitarians tend to sacrifice *earlier* rather than later generations. This is due to the conjunction of two features.

The first feature is that increasing productivity requires technological investment – broadly construed – which in turn *takes time*. Investment comes first and benefits – if any – only come later. The current generation tightens its belt to fund blue-sky research. Future generations reap the rewards. Not only will the benefits from investment only emerge in the future; they will also be stuck in the future. Mortality and the irreversibility of time will prevent future people from sharing them with their predecessors. This is the second feature. Assuming here that the backward sharing of future benefits is unachievable, the necessary duration of investment coupled with the irreversibility of time opens the gate to a potential justification for inequality between generations. In short, you cannot harvest a long-term crop on the day you sowed it. And when the harvest season comes, the sowing generation has died. As a result, if you ought to contribute to maximizing cross-generational well-being, you will end up transferring more potential for well-being to the next generation than you inherited yourself. This is the core message.

Some factors may of course mitigate such a conclusion, and others worsen it.[6] Let me just make two points here. First, some of the benefits may already be reaped during an investing generation's own lifetime. Nevertheless, the technological options transferred to the next generation will still be enriched compared to the ones we inherited. Second, couldn't an investing generation "borrow" from the future or pay itself anticipatively?[7] Consider two options. If it were through running a public debt, there would still be a group *in the present* – albeit from another country – that would incur the costs from lending the money today. If it were through consuming more non-renewable resources today than we would otherwise be entitled to, in exchange for more efficient future technologies, we run the risk of losing on one side what we gain on the other. Also, if such non-renewable resources are likely to be used less efficiently than if we were waiting for the new technology to become available, paying ourselves in this way would amount to an inefficient timing of energy consumption. As a result, it would clash with the requirement of maximizing cross-generational well-being.

To sum up, "better future" is clearly distinct from "non-decline." It is at home with a utilitarian approach. While impartial toward the various generations, the latter may justify the sacrifice of earlier generations for the sake of "us all," out of concern for cross-generational well-being maximization. It builds on two features of the intergenerational world: investment takes time, and benefits arising in the future cannot be shared back with the present for all those who died in the meantime. Yet concern for sacrificing some generations in the name of others may lead the reader to turn to alternative views.

View 3: having enough
The third view is again quite different. While common for those familiar with the sustainability literature, it can be backed by still another conception of justice: sufficientarianism. All views about justice tell us something about whether we are *doing* enough for others. Yet *sufficientarianism* says that it is only once all *have* enough that we have *done* enough.[8] Consider two successive generations and let us assume constant population size. Justice requires that each generation has *enough* of some x – for instance, enough to cover its members' basic needs. This is a possible interpretation of the Brundtland definition of sustainable development, to which I return below.

Consider first a generation that inherited a basket of natural resources and technology able to cover *way more* than the basic needs of its population – say, ten times more. The "having enough" view would then clearly *authorize savings*, provided that the investments needed do not threaten covering the basic needs of the *current* generation's members. It would also *authorize dis-savings*, provided that the next generation would still have enough. In our "ten times more than basic needs require" scenario, this would allow this generation to squander 90 per cent of what it inherited.

Consider an alternative scenario under which a generation inherited *just enough* to cover its own basic needs. In this case, *dis-savings are prohibited* because we would otherwise put the next generation below threshold. *Savings are also prohibited.* Otherwise, the investments required are likely to put members of the *current* generation below the sufficiency threshold. Note, however, that "quick and lasting returns on investments," i.e. those that generate net benefits for the investing generation itself and potentially as well for future ones, can render generational savings and keeping the current generation afloat compatible, especially if "having enough" is broadly understood across people's entire lifetime. Yet we can see that even in the presence of such types of returns, the margin remains narrow, and may not allow for massive savings. This anticipates our discussion of the fourth view below.

In addition, the sufficientarian view seems less compatible with *compulsory savings or dis-savings*. Actually, no plausible view so far has commanded *compulsory dis-saving*, at least if we leave aside population decline or the possibility of "future external and positive shocks" – two significant caveats. And it is also unlikely that a "having enough" view would render *savings compulsory* out of concern for the *next* generation's basic needs, unless we take into account circumstances of the type we just mentioned.

In a nutshell, the sufficientarian account provides us with an intuition that sounds familiar to many. It belongs to a distinct threshold-based family of views that associates justice with sufficiency. It clearly carries implications that differ from the two previous views when it comes to generational savings and dis-savings. Such implications are more complex to work out. This complexity results from the interaction under such a sufficiency view between an independently defined sufficiency threshold and the efforts expected from the current generation. These efforts depend on the gap between what the sufficiency standard requires and what the current generation happens to have inherited. Yet the possibility of significant squandering authorized by sufficientarianism remains puzzling. And the very fact that sufficientarianism may not match the demands of our general view about justice invites us to seek alternatives too.

View 4: narrow path

To complete the picture, there is a fourth alternative that is both intriguing and distinctive.[9] In line with the "non-decline" and the "better future" views, it tends to prohibit generational dis-savings. However, contrary to these views, it also tends to *prohibit* generational savings, for reasons that are akin to the ones just discussed in the "having enough" section. In short, it defines a narrow path according to which it is unfair both to dis-save and to save as a generation, even if, as we will see, it is not unfair toward the same groups in both cases.

One account of justice seems able to support such a narrow path: *leximin egalitarianism.* This view brings together several intuitions. The key intuition is that instead of caring about inequality as such, leximin (or "lexical maximin") cares about maximizing the situation of the least well-off, and then about the second least well-off, etc., lexicographically. The label refers to a "lexicographic priority" (*lexi-*) and to maximizing the situation of the least well-off (*-min*).[10] As is the case with utilitarians, this special kind of egalitarianism allows for departures from equality and cares about maximization. However, it only accepts departures from equality if the efficiency gains that such departures allow improve the situation of the least well-off members in society. As is the case with sufficientarians, this special kind of egalitarianism cares about the least well-off. However, it does not rest content with the fact that they would end up being sufficiently well-off. It claims that we should put in place policies that would make them *maximally* well-off. Like sufficientarianism, the "narrow path" view cares about how much it costs to the *current* least well-off to engage in a generational savings path – the opportunity cost for them. However, unlike for sufficientarianism, it leaves less room for savings, as the latter would only be allowed if the situation of the currently least well-off could not be improved any more. Along the same line, it would not be as open to dis-savings and squandering as sufficientarianism, for it cares about maximally improving the situation of the future least well-off too. Hence, the path is narrower for leximin egalitarians than for sufficientarians.

Endorsing "narrow path" leads to a major challenge to the possibility and acceptability of *accumulation* from one generation to the next. This challenge rests on grounds of justice. This is disturbing. What could possibly be unfair about handing on a *better* world to the next generation? Isn't it better for them if they get something better? At this stage, it is very important to understand both how this type of objection to accumulation differs from other ones and why intergenerational justice would object to accumulation.

Let me first clarify how it differs from other claims. A first set of objections to accumulation has to do with the extent to which it tends to be intensive in non-renewable natural resources. We may be concerned about the fact that resource-intensive accumulation cannot continue indefinitely into the future at this rate and that it would only be acceptable if it could. We may be preoccupied about the environmental externalities of extracting natural resources, such as the impact on climate of burning fossil fuels. We may worry about the degree to which extracting more natural resources intensifies the democracy deficit of resource-rich countries. While these three concerns ought to be taken seriously, none of them characterizes what is at the heart of "narrow path" as defined here.

A second set of objections to wealth accumulation points to the fact that the increase in productive potential can be a problem *even if*, by some quirk, we somehow managed to fully "decouple" it from an increase in natural resource extraction. One worry would still be that the centrality of any accumulation goal – not merely one focusing on GDP increase – renders it *illiberal*,[11] as this goal may lack neutrality toward conceptions of the good life for which accumulation is inessential or counterproductive if we want to run meaningful lives. Relatedly, even if one is not a liberal, one may worry that wealth accumulation may be vain in terms of the good life. A different worry is that accumulation, even if it were not resource-intensive, presupposes an increase in inequalities because of the incentive schemes it generally requires. One concern is that increasing inequalities may cancel out the benefit of accumulation in terms of well-being. Data indicate that the effect of wealth accumulation on well-being increase is at best limited, as larger inequalities pull aggregate well-being down through relative-wealth-sensitivity phenomena. Owning a bike is likely to make you feel happier in a society in which your neighbors also own a bike than in one in which they all own luxury cars.

The driving force of the "narrow path" view differs from the concerns just listed, including those worried specifically about rising inequalities usually associated with wealth accumulation. And while this driving concern is about the unjust nature of some intergenerational transfers, it actually turns out not to reflect a concern about *intergenerational* justice in the strict sense – which echoes our discussion in the book's introduction. For when we object to transferring more to the next generation than we inherited from the previous one, we actually question whether a given generation is being fair toward its *own* members, as opposed to past or future generations. Yet this is still an intergenerational justice concern in the broad sense, for what we are ultimately concerned about is justice *across* generations rather than between generations taken as black boxes. Worries about an intergenerational transfer driven by a concern for some of the members of our own generation fits, then, perfectly well within this.

The worry that the "narrow path" view reflects was already present in the "having enough" view. It is magnified here by the maximizing feature present in leximin egalitarianism – or possibly in related views such as Gini prioritarianism.[12] Transferring stuff to the next generation imposes costs on us, especially opportunity costs on the poorest among us. If we have a surplus compared to what we inherited, we should allocate it to our own least well-off members rather than the next generation as a whole. If each generation does so, our intergenerational path will be such that the least well-off groups across the generations, whichever generation they are part of, will be better off than the least well-off groups under a scenario allowing for generational savings. Importantly enough, this "mind your own least well-off" slogan is not driven by any form of generationalism. It is driven instead by an intergenerationally impartial concern for selecting the cross-generational path such that the least well-off individuals across the generations will be as well-off as possible.

Having clarified the underlying rationale, the next question is whether we are really bound to remain stuck forever with our current level of wealth. Those willing to stick to some priority for the least well-off may nevertheless want to explore ways of rendering our range of acceptable trajectories less narrow than "narrow path." Here are four possible directions to explore.

First, isn't it realistic to expect today's least well-off to actually agree on some accumulation? Many parents tighten their belts for their own children, especially when they are very poor. They do so for their own kids against a background of intragenerational inequalities that are *given*. Yet were such poor parents given the chance of loosening their belts, having received the guarantee that inequalities within their kids' generation would be much smaller than they currently are, would their attitude remain the same? I doubt it.

Second, can't some early returns from investment benefit both future people (because such returns will last) and the current least well-off (because they come early)? Yes. The transmission of temporally *non-rival* goods (new technology) to the next generation does not necessarily prevent us from already using them today. But we need to ensure that these early returns on technological investments are large enough for the current least well-off to be compensated for the opportunity cost of their initial development. In addition, if we anticipate better technology being transferred to the next generation, we could to some degree compensate this through consuming more non-renewable natural resources. However, we pointed to the issue of efficient timing of such consumption, which has possible repercussions for the least well-off.

Third, future and predictable external shocks as well as population increase also matter. Both of them not only allow for but even *require generational savings* (per capita) if future shocks are negative or if population increases. And they would actually *require dis-savings* if future shocks were positive or if population decreased.

The "early returns" and "future external shocks" points both suggest that there might actually be room for departing from a strict prohibition on savings – and even from one on dis-savings – within the framework of a leximin egalitarian view that aims at maximizing the situation of the least well-off. While the path would remain narrow, it would not be as narrow as initially stated. Let me conclude with a *fourth* possible consideration. Here, we would broaden the path by revising our principles of justice rather than by pointing to unnoticed features of the intergenerational world. Concretely, we could relax the priority for the least well-off, leaving room for inequalities increases *even if* they do not benefit the least well-off. This would broaden our path provided that associated aggregate benefits for the next generation as a whole are major. We would then move away from the "narrow path" view, going somewhere in the direction of "better future."

In a nutshell, "narrow path," like "non-decline" and "better future," prohibits dis-savings in principle. It also prohibits savings in general, in a more radical manner than "having enough." I linked it to a specific view about justice, i.e. leximin egalitarianism. I also stressed how the leximin logic underlying "narrow path" differs from other views opposed to accumulation. Finally, I identified different ways in which the prohibition on savings can be softened or reversed.

***

What is the takeaway message from exploring these four views? It is twofold. First, there are significant differences between them. Second, each of them can be backed with an underlying general theory of justice. What matters is to understand how we derive our "savings/dis-savings" principles from these theories of justice.

How should the reader, then, go from here to making up her own mind about which of these four positions – if any – to adopt on the matter? One way is to aim at some form of "reflective equilibrium" – as Rawls would call it.[13] The method is simple. It takes as a starting point any normative intuition you may have about specific issues – such as "selling votes should be prohibited" or "we should not let the Georgian language die" – or general principles that you may be committed to – such as "goods with features

w or x should not be commodified" or "a language should be kept alive if y or z." You can start at a low or at a high level of generality (specific judgment vs. general principle). The idea is to confront a variety of specific judgments and general principles until they all become compatible with each other ("equilibrium") and until we fully understand which principles our specific judgments are reflecting ("reflective"). The method serves both a *discovery* and a *critical* purpose. It helps you to discover your position on issue w in case you are unsure or haven't thought about it yet. It does so based on a confrontation with the position that you may already have on issue x or on principle y. It also forces you to ask yourself whether your position on issue x makes sense once confronted with your position on the other issue, z, through the angle of principle y. You will have to readjust your judgments and reformulate your principles until you reach a coherent set. In the present case, you should compare the four intergenerational views and their underlying logic with specific intuitions you may have and with general principles of justice that you would be ready to adopt, including beyond the intergenerational realm.

As far as I am concerned, the possibility of net transfers is key to any theory of justice, which makes me drop the reciprocity view. An exclusive concern for maximizing an aggregate without sufficient weight given to distributive patterns makes me reject the second view. The third one rests on a sufficiency view that, at least if the threshold remains basic and is uncomplemented by additional concerns for justice, is insufficient to meet what I consider to be the demands of fair distribution. I am then left with some version of "narrow path," more or less strictly construed, involving a more or less strict priority for the least well-off, possibly combined with a sufficientarian component. And I remain open to finer descriptions of the intergenerational world that would allow us to relax the prohibition on savings while sticking to a significant priority for the least well-off. The surprise is that while our practical concern tends to be dominated by the fear of not doing enough for the future, the present theoretical challenge is about how to create normative space for *entitling* us to do *more* for the future.

Should generational inheritance rule?

Having presented four options and their internal logic, let me now zoom out to reflect on the "savings/dis-savings" framing. I want to consider the role played by *what (and how much) we inherit* in the way we frame obligations to the next generation(s). Doubts arise from three sources. First, isn't there some degree of arbitrariness in the level that we inherited? If so, why should it play such a significant role in defining what we owe the future? Second, and relatedly, in the context of overlapping generations, why should the previous generation set the standard, as opposed to several generations deliberating about what the standard should be? Third, are the opportunities we enjoy throughout the course of our lives properly described as mostly inherited from the previous generation? If not, why frame things in terms of generational savings/dis-savings and why give such a central role to generational inheritance?

Who should set the standard? Cleanliness rules
To address our threefold worry, let me refer to a *cleronomic* (or "inheritance-ruled") framing as one that assigns a "core" role to what (and how much) we inherited in setting the standard about what (and how much) we owe the next generation(s). "Cleronomic" comes from the Greek "kleros" and "nomos" and means here "ruled by what we inherited." I am not intending to deny the importance of what we inherited in our wealth. I am concerned about a too exclusive focus on it. A twofold question arises: what does an inheritance-ruled perspective *mean* and what (if anything) is *wrong* with it? After a detour

through the field of cleanliness rules, I will come back to our four intergenerational views.

Consider cleanliness rules for spaces with *successive users* – a possible inspiration for principles of intergenerational justice. Here is one:

Please leave the place in a state *at least as clean as* the one in which you found it.

Under this rule, which I take to be paradigmatically inheritance-ruled, if the place happens to be unbearably dirty and if you don't care about it for yourself, there is no problem in transferring it in such a bad state to the next users. In contrast, if the place has been obsessively kept in a state that is unnecessarily clean, you should stick to that standard too, even if it involves huge efforts to hold on to what seems epidemiologically absurd. There is a sense in which the level of cleanliness that we inherited is relatively arbitrary, as these two scenarios illustrate. This invites the following observations.

First, each user is bound to stick to the standard of the previous one, rather than to her own. This amounts to a "one-beat delay" (or "staggered") normativity. Yet why trust the previous generation more than the current one? Of course, the rule aims at having more bite than a mere "Please leave the space (in a state as clean) as you wish" or "Please leave the space (in a state as clean) as you would wish to have found it." Note that in the latter case, hypothetical self-imposition is supposed to add one degree of safeguard to the "as you wish" version. Yet the "at least as clean" rule gains bite at the cost of saying "Please leave the space (in a state as clean) as the previous generation wished." The previous generation may of course have done things right. However, it may also have disregarded its intergenerational duties. Even in the latter case, our cleanliness rule sticks to what the previous generation left us as a standard.

In fact, what looks like a substantive standard rather amounts to a decision procedure that allocates the full standard-setting power to the previous generation. This differs from the kind of arbitrariness encountered, for instance, in cases of equality among contemporaries. Of course, the wealth levels that we are able to reach at a given point in history also depend on the moment in history at which we happen to live, as well as on the ability and willingness to work of our contemporaries. This admittedly also involves some level of arbitrariness that egalitarians need to accept. Yet what happens with the "at least as clean" rule is that it is the willingness to bequeath of the previous generation that is actually the core element that determines what the current generation owes the next one.

In addition, the "at least as clean" rule does not necessarily reflect any "fair effort" standard. Admittedly, not forcing us to clean up the mess in a case where we inherit a very dirty environment spares us overdemanding duties. In addition, not allowing the cleanliness state to go down also distributes the cleaning effort across generations, avoiding one of them being bound to engage in taking up the cumulated slack at some point. Yet having to stick to obsessive levels of cleanliness set at some point by a maniac generation may be unacceptably burdensome for a long series of generations. In the end, under this rule, and besides the possibility of rendering the place even cleaner, the current generation's only – yet non-negligible – margin rests with the *interpretation* of what "cleanliness" amounts to – which connects with our discussion about "metrics" in the next chapter.

I have just stressed serious problems associated with cleronomicity. I will re-examine our four principles of intergenerational justice from that angle and explore the possibility of alternative framings. Before that, let me further secure a firmer understanding of what I mean by "cleronomic" or "inheritance-ruled." Consider three alternative cleanliness rules:

Please leave the place ...

... in a state as clean as the *average* one in which the last *five* generations found it.

... in a state *cleaner* than the average one in which the last five generations found it.

... in the *cleanest* state in which one of the last five generations found it.

My purpose is not to compare these rules' respective properties. Instead, I aim to find out whether each of them qualifies as cleronomic, as inheritance-ruled, i.e. whether what we inherited plays a *central role* in defining what we owe the next generation. Or better, are some of them *more or less* cleronomic than others? Here are two thoughts.

First, in formulating these three alternative cleanliness rules, I shifted the focus from what is inherited from the *very last* generation to what the *five last* generations bequeathed (on average) to their respective successors. This renders the reference level slightly less arbitrary and less sensitive to generational fluctuations. Still, what our predecessors bequeathed collectively continues to play a major role in defining what we owe the future. Hence, these three alternatives can still be said to be significantly cleronomic, despite having broadened the group of decisive generations. The second idea is that the third of these alternative rules picks the *highest* bequest among the last five generations. Hence, it adds an important requirement, perhaps taking that level as a feasibility indicator. Still, even that third alternative rule remains strongly inheritance-ruled. For what one of the five last generations bequeathed still plays a major standard-definition role.

In short, these three alternative rules remain strongly cleronomic despite not concentrating exclusively on the last generation or not sticking to an "at least as clean" idea. I hope to have successfully conveyed the sense that relying on the (few) last generation(s) for standard setting involves a significant degree of arbitrariness.

Generational inheritance: standard or constraint?

I still have a few tasks ahead. First, I wish to show that one of the four views discussed earlier in the chapter is significantly *less* inheritance-ruled than the others, even if that view retains some degree of cleronomicity. Second, I aim to check whether some of the other four views about intergenerational justice *can* also be rephrased in less cleronomic terms. Third, I will come back to whether it is *desirable* to drop the inheritance-ruled perspective as much as possible.

I begin with the first task. The best entry point to understand what a less cleronomic framing amounts to consists in returning to the "having enough" view (sufficientarianism). I stressed the complexity of its relationship with savings/dis-savings language. Such complexity arises from the fact that the sufficientarian view's heart is non-cleronomic. Considering its "basic needs" version, the latter notion requires an account of what is supposed to be essential for a human being. This account does not primarily depend on what the previous generations happen to have left us. And still, even for such a view, there are ways in which what we inherited plays a significant role. The degree to which we are able to meet our own basic needs depends a lot on how much we inherited. And whether we can meet the needs of the next generation while covering our own also depends on what the previous generations left us.[14] While none of this means that how much we inherited should be seen as a *standard*, it certainly means that generational inheritance acts as a feasibility *constraint* on what we owe the future. Here, I assume – which is not self-evident – that constraints and standards differ in kind. And I conjecture that presenting as a constraint something that was initially seen as a standard can make a difference in how we approach things, and in how we act as a consequence. This suggests a twofold conclusion. First, "having enough" definitely involves a non-cleronomic standard. Second, "having enough" cannot fully ignore what we inherited in defining what we owe the future.

The second task is to find out whether the other three views on intergenerational justice can also be reformulated in less cleronomic terms. Consider utilitarianism. Remember that what is crucial is to maximize the total level of well-being across current and future generations taken as a whole. What is feasible to achieve depends in part on what we inherited. However, it will also depend on other factors: what we manage to achieve from now on, the skills that people are willing to develop, the effort that they are able to deploy, natural phenomena that are likely to occur, etc. Hence, whether our lives go well does not fully depend on what our ancestors did. And whether the life of the next generation will go well may also depend on natural phenomena such as the fall of a comet, the occurrence of which does not necessarily need to be presented as the result of what we inherited and the predictability of which may affect what we owe the future. This would be the case for a comet expected today to fall on Earth in sixty years. Hence, here is a possible non-cleronomic account of what utilitarianism requires: "each generation owes the next one what will maximize well-being *from now on.*" The focus is not so much on whether more or less "stuff" will end up being transferred to the future compared with what we inherited. The focus is rather on whether we transfer the right amount to maximize well-being *from now on.*

Such a "forward-looking" account – which should include the entire life of all the currently alive and future generations – potentially gives a less central role to what we inherited. And it carries us beyond merely expecting us to transfer "more than we inherited" to the future, allowing us to assess "*how much* more" is expected. This alternative framing does not convey the sense that the actions of the previous generations provide us with a standard or even play the central role in deciding what we owe the next generation.

Along the same lines, leximin egalitarianism, our last view, could simply be framed as: "each generation owes the next one what is compatible with maximizing the situation of the least well-off *from now on.*" Note here that, because of the "entire-life" perspective spelled out in the introduction, "from now on" should be interpreted in the leximin case as "starting from the birth of the currently existing generations." In contrast, "from now on" can be interpreted literally in the utilitarian case, since the latter is not concerned about equalizing over complete lives.

We are then left with the first view, the reciprocity-based one. It *cannot* be reframed in non-cleronomic terms. Cleronomicity is at the heart of its DNA. It is what one generation transferred to us that is supposed to trigger an obligation to reciprocate and define the level expected. Since the view is "commutative," what one generation has done to us – be it framed in output or in effort terms – provides a standard as opposed to a mere constraint.

Approaching things from the angle of cleronomicity allows us to understand "having enough" (sufficientarian) and "non-decline" (reciprocity-based) as being located at opposite ends of a spectrum, the former being the least "inheritance-ruled" whereas the latter is deeply inheritance-ruled. As to "better future" (utilitarianism) and "narrow path" (leximin egalitarianism), they can be reframed in ways that are less inheritance-ruled. The respective rules might then be synoptically presented and slightly reordered as follows:

G1 should transfer to G2 ...

... at least as much as it inherited from G0 (reciprocity).
... what would maximize total well-being from now on (utilitarianism).
... what would be best for the least well-off from now on (leximin egalitarianism).
... what would allow covering the basic needs of all from now on (sufficientarianism).

Here, the reference to what we inherited only remains explicit in the first account. The wide presence of reciprocity logic in public debate (e.g. in framing retirement pension duties) may partly explain our tendency to frame things in inheritance-ruled terms. Once we realize this, we can envisage more "from now on," forward-looking accounts of our obligations to the future. This opens up possible thinking about putting into perspective the relative importance of what we inherited from the past compared with our own ability to open possibilities for the future, or the importance of future exogenous events the predictability of which might evolve over time. This also allows us to depart from a somewhat "artificial" account of the expected fall of a comet or the predicted eruption of a volcano as being "inherited from our parents." It allows us as well to depart from an account that sticks to what was possible when the previous generation died to define what we owe the future, in case new technology (or other new non-rival goods) enables us to address key challenges much more easily. In short, moving away from an inheritance-ruled, cleronomic framing forces us to be more explicit about our real standard and about the degree to which facts other than generational inheritance should enter the picture.

In the end, can we do without an account of what we inherited from the previous generation? Not entirely, because generational inheritance is likely to remain a very important feasibility constraint. Yet we are invited to think more carefully about the degree to which what we inherited constrains our options. And framing our inheritance as a feasibility constraint rather than as a standard also allows us to reframe our intergenerational standards. It allows us as well to see "non-decline" and "having enough" as being located at opposite ends of the cleronomicity spectrum. This is quite intriguing because they also happen to match to some extent the two most common understandings of "sustainability," a topic to which we now turn.

Justice without sustainability (and conversely)?

I have just presented several possible accounts of intergenerational justice. I stressed that, for three of them at least, there was room for a less cleronomic framing. In the previous section, I also defended the idea that the non-identity problem did not force us to renounce framing our demands in terms of intergenerational justice. And yet some may still object that emphasizing justice entirely misses the point about what should most concern us about the future. The real issue would be the very survival of life on Earth or, more narrowly, the risk of extinction of humankind. Also, stressing the key importance of continuing the human adventure may be approached axiologically (the undesirability of extinction) or morally (the immorality of extinction). None of these necessarily invokes the idea of justice, and some might even want to suggest that facing existential risks and avoiding human extinction should prevail over being intergenerationally fair, for instance through sacrificing current people in one way or another.[15] While concerns about (human) extinction seem crucial to me, I think that they can be treated as an issue of justice to some extent. Let me add two thoughts at this stage.

First, as to the meaning of our lives, I will assume that since humankind will most likely come to an end at *some* point (in a few billion years if we are very optimistic), whether our existence makes sense should not fully depend on how long the human adventure will last. The same holds at the individual level: accounts of the meaning of our existence should take our individual mortality seriously, and not let this meaning fully depend on followers.

Second, I will come back in the next chapter to whether we have a *duty* to continue the human adventure, which entails a generational duty to procreate. The key point at this stage is rather to understand the difference between caring about the further continuation of humankind and caring about the *possibility* of such a continuation ("possibilism"). It is one thing to ensure that coming generations enjoy living conditions that don't render it impossible to engender further generations if they still find it meaningful to do so. It is quite another to see the continuation of humankind as something desirable or even required.

I understand that allowing each generation to be the last generation gives a lot of power to each generation. It would be entitled to end alone the human adventure. But we ought not to transform our successors into our "meaning slaves." They should not be expected to procreate for the "mere" sake of preserving the meaningfulness of their ancestors' own project. Caring about existential risks for the future is actually compatible with both the "possibilist" and the "meaninglessness without a future" ideas. Yet it is important to keep their difference in mind.

Here, I approach these matters from a specific angle, by confronting intergenerational justice with *sustainability*.[16] The latter also touches on the idea of the continuation of humankind and the possibility of such continuation. The issue is whether what drives our concern for the present and future should be fairness between generations or, rather, sustainability, and whether they differ from one another. I will ask whether a way of life can be sustainable *without* being intergenerationally just (sufficiency) and whether it can be intergenerationally just *without* being sustainable (necessity).[17]

While sustainability has come to refer these days to pretty much everything that people positively value, it is worth considering its core semantic connotations through returning to its etymology. In the verb "sustaining," "-taining" comes from the Latin "tenere." The latter refers to "holding with the hand," but also to *holding on to*, which stresses a sense of duration (as in "durability"). Both connotations are also present in "maintaining," the French "main" meaning "hand." As to the prefix "sus-," it comes from the Latin "sub" and means "from underneath." It echoes "enter-taining," which initially referred to the idea of mutual ("inter") support, later leading to the French "entretenir," which means to maintain.[18]

Hence, the rich etymology of "sustainability" captures some of its key dimensions: a reference to the ability to last through time ("durability"), the ability to provide for the underlying conditions supporting such permanence ("supportability"), the ability to preserve something in a good or constant state ("maintainability"), and the ability to cover people's needs ("entertainability"). In addition, for philosophers, sustainability may also echo a concern for "generalizability" over time – as when we care about how many planets would be needed if all were to adopt the same consumption pattern as ours.

Non-decline vs. sufficientarian sustainability

Consider the sustainability of a practice, understood in the descriptive sense of its ability to be sustained, to last for a long time. Some undesirable practices, such as physical violence, could unfortunately last for generations ahead. Other practices may not be repeatable while not necessarily being undesirable. Think about consuming a non-renewable resource that is not durable, the consumption of which is only possible once. Hence, some undesirable practices are sustainable and some non-sustainable practices are desirable.

This indicates that we need more than a descriptive concept of sustainability. A normative account should tell us why and when our ability to sustain a way of life or a practice into the future should be seen as a necessary requirement for its desirability or moral acceptability. It should also tell us what should be sustained and why. I hope to contribute to the latter dimension here, and to help in understanding the relationship between sustainability and justice. If we look at the sustainability literature, there seem to be two main options for a core normative concept of sustainability: "non-decline" and "having enough." Let us begin with two *non-decline* definitions of sustainability:

> *Asheim:* "Any non-decreasing utility stream is sustainable – according to any common definition of the notion of sustainable."[19]

> *Barry:* "The core concept of sustainability is ... that there is some X whose value should be maintained, in as far as it lies within our power to do so, into the indefinite future."[20]

Non-decline sustainability demands that a level L of a valuable X be maintained into the indefinite future. Asheim equates X with utility here whereas Barry remains open in that respect. Both specify that L should not decline. They don't tell us where to locate L and it does not even seem that we should necessarily take as a reference point the L *inherited* from the previous generation. Hence, non-decline sustainability seems broader than non-decline justice as defined above. In a first approximation, non-decline justice understood in cleronomic terms can be seen as a subspecies of non-decline sustainability.

Contrast these non-decline definitions of sustainability with an alternative definition from the Brundtland Commission. It claims that development is sustainable if it "meets the needs of the present without compromising the ability of future generations to meet their own needs."[21] This connects with the "having enough" approach of justice, at least if we accept reading "needs" as "basic needs." We are dealing here with a threshold view that simultaneously defines a metrics and a level: basic needs. It does not coincide with a cleronomic non-decline view that would assess non-decline from the level of x that we inherited. Yet the Brundtland account could also fit within Barry's definition if we accept replacing "x" with "the means to cover basic needs." This implies that cleronomic, non-decline justice and sufficientarian, basic-needs sustainability could both be read as subspecies of Barry's general definition of sustainability.

Where to go from here? Claiming that something should be edible, visible, or affordable does not entail that it should respectively be eaten, seen, or bought. In a similar vein, requiring that some x be sustain*able* does not entail that it should be sustain*ed*, maintained, kept alive. In a first approximation, sustainability seems to merely require the possibility of sustenance, the "power" to sustain – in Barry's terms. Asheim is right to claim that the fact that some x was sustained *indicates* that it was sustainable. Yet when Barry claims that sustainability requires that something should be maintained into the future, he might be going one step too far. At first sight, the duty of sustainability might not entail any duty of sustenance.

Consider then the metrics of sustainability, i.e. "sustainability of what?" Imagine that you hold a view about justice such that each generation owes the next generation a given level of x. This level itself can be defined in "opportunity" terms. By this, I mean for instance "opportunity for welfare" instead of "welfare," or "productive potential" rather than "actual production." It could *seem* that the more we define the metrics of our theory of justice in such "possibilist" terms, the more the demands of justice and sustainability will coincide. Yet a difference remains. Think about a non-decline approach. My duty of justice as a generation could mean that I owe the next generation a productive potential that is not lower than the one I inherited. A related view about my duty of sustainability will require that I owe the next generation a productive potential such that it will be *able* to transfer at least the same to *its own successor* – in the spirit of the indirect strategy mentioned in the previous chapter. We said that ensuring that a given x *can be* sustained does not entail that this same x *should be* sustained. Yet we now understand that "sustainability of x" still implies that something *should be* sustained. Crucially, it is not x as such but rather the possibility for the next generation to transfer x in turn to its own successors. Hence, the duty of sustainability entails a duty to sustain. However, both duties have distinct – though related – objects. The latter is a duty to sustain the possibility to sustain.

Note that a more demanding duty of sustainability could require making sure that the next generation be able to transfer the relevant level of x to its successor *while enjoying it for itself too.* It is unclear whether the latter concern – explicit in the Brundtland definition – is required by sustainability itself or whether it results from the addition of extra demands of justice. There could be a lax concept of sustainability such that some level of x could be sustained into the remote future provided that intermediary generations sacrifice themselves, including to the point of having to remain below this level of x. Under this concept, sustainability would be preserved, despite violating intergenerational fairness in one sense, namely despite what I will refer to below as "temporary" decline.[22]

All this shows that justice intuitions are already built in to some accounts of sustainability. For analytical purposes, it is best to adopt a not-too-rich definition of sustainability, to allow us to understand how it interacts with the various components and accounts of inter-generational justice. I will use a non-decline version of a duty of sustainability that is normative, cleronomic, and sequential, that rejects the possibility of temporary decline, while not committing to any specific metrics. On such grounds, let us look at whether we can have intergen-erational justice without sustainability, and conversely. Here is our starting point:

Non-decline sustainability
Each generation owes the next generation a level of x at least equivalent to the level it inherited from the previous generation *and* sufficient to allow the next generation to transfer at least the same level of x in turn to its own successors.

Sustainability without justice
Could the demands of sustainability be satisfied without those of intergenerational justice being met? Some of the possible divergences are already put aside by our choice of definition. Our definition of non-decline sustainability converges with a non-decline account of justice on a

variety of fronts: it is inheritance-ruled, it is assumed to use the same metrics, and it rejects "temporary" decline.

This being said, when we talk about a non-declining *stream* of well-being, we know that at each of the successive periods, the total amount of utility is non-declining. We might be tempted to conclude that if there is a stock of material resources and technology – broadly understood – that is constant (per capita) across the successive *periods* of time, then both non-decline sustainability and non-decline justice are met. Yet this is not necessarily the case. It all depends on how the actual opportunities for well-being are distributed across the various coexisting generations over their respective lives.

A definition that would replace "generation" with "period" in our sustainability definition ("Each period owes the next period … ") would disregard the possibility of sacrificed and golden generations. This goes beyond the mere idea of a temporary decline. Some generations may be sacrificed despite the constancy in the total amount of well-being across the successive periods. The possibility of sacrificed and golden generations is a significant problem of justice. It is not captured whenever sustainability focuses on comparing successive *periods* without looking at the lifetime effect of their internal inequalities on the generations at stake.

Hence, non-decline definitions of sustainability that focus on periods of time rather than generations may not meet the demands of non-decline intergenerational justice, as the latter applies to the entire lifetime of successive generations. This is a first reason why there could be sustainability without justice. And sustainability may even be too demanding, as one may imagine temporary declines of the relevant x that do not lead to any inequalities over entire lives between the coexisting cohorts. This very last point anticipates the next section, devoted to whether there can be intergenerational justice without sustainability.

There is a second possible source of disjunction. Non-decline sustainability does not meet the demands of the intergenerational justice accounts that require more than mere non-decline. "Better future" clearly requires generational savings on top. "Having enough" may require generational savings or dis-savings depending on the circumstances described above. As to "narrow path," it prohibits generational savings. Hence, these three non-decline accounts of intergenerational justice have reasons to consider non-decline sustainability as an *insufficient* account of intergenerational justice. Whenever an account departs from merely authorizing generational savings, it will diverge from the demands of non-decline sustainability. And there would be further grounds for divergence if we hadn't already built in, within the definition of non-decline sustainability, some of the features that bring it closer to an account of non-decline justice.

Justice without sustainability
I have shown why an intergenerational path could be sustainable *without being fair*. This comes either from adopting a period-focused (rather than "generation-focused") definition of sustainability, or from endorsing a definition of intergenerational justice that requires more than non-decline. Let us find out about the reverse: can an unsustainable way of life be intergenerationally fair? I will approach it from three angles.

First, any theory of intergenerational justice that allows for – or even imposes in some cases – generational *dis-savings* violates non-decline sustainability. This is the case of the "having enough" view. It allows for dis-savings when there is more than enough to cover the basic needs of the current and the next generation(s). It is also the case for "narrow path," whenever we have reasons to think that a current exogenous and negative shock – like an exceptional volcano eruption – will not repeat itself in the predictable future. In that case, not going for dis-savings would disadvantage current people, and the least well-off among them. Hence, for "having enough" and "narrow path," in the circumstances that we identified, non-decline sustainability should be violated if we care about justice.

Second, consider now the "non-decline" and the "narrow path" views of justice in the absence of any external shocks. Under the indirect strategy that we alluded to earlier – let's label it "the right to procreate fairly" – non-decline sustainability is a necessary requirement of justice. This strategy joins two normative claims.[23] The first claim says that as part of what we owe to the next generation, there is an obligation *not to prevent* the next generation from fulfilling its own duties of intergenerational justice toward its own descendants – understood as birth cohorts. Let's label this first claim "their duties are my duties." The second claim says that what we owe the next generation includes the obligation not to impede it from having children. Let's label this second claim "their right to procreate." Joining the two claims, we *could* have a sustainability requirement endogenizing obligations of justice to the next-but-one generation as part of our obligations to our direct successors. The idea is that it is only right for me to reproduce if I can guarantee for the next generation the conditions for it exercising the same right in turn, and so on. The interesting question is under which conditions the demands of this approach could be met.

The plausibility of this strategy depends on how we interpret the two claims. We formulated the "their duties are my duties" claim in negative terms ("not to prevent"). But of course, this may include positive obligations. For instance, it means that if there are enough non-renewable resources for two extra generations, I should not simply leave enough to reach the level of x of the next generation, irrespective of what it owes its own children. The problem is that if this strategy is used ad infinitum, it might end up being as demanding as a "better future" view under certain interpretations, were our duties to be interpreted as more than negative obligations – which they should be.[24]

The other possible source of skepticism toward the "right to procreate fairly" strategy is that demandingness could also come from not capping the right to procreate. Imagine that the next generation intends to double its birth rate compared to ours. In that case, it would mean that for sustainability to be preserved, were it interpreted in a *per capita* manner and in line with the "their duties are my duties" intuition, the current generation should probably double what it owes the next generation in absolute terms, regardless of whether it itself values a lower birth rate. This as such does not necessarily disalign non-decline justice and non-decline sustainability, provided that *both* are defined in per capita terms, that we define the content of the right to procreate in the same terms, and that non-decline justice endorses the "their duties are my duties" view. So, the "right to procreate fairly" strategy offers a promising avenue to align the demands of non-decline sustainability and non-decline justice. And to that extent, we could claim that any view that rejects the possibility of generational dis-savings could require non-decline sustainability as a necessary requirement.

Third, there is a final source of divergence between justice and sustainability. Imagine that the substitutability of non-renewable resources with technology is limited. This opens the possibility that we unavoidably belong to a *cake-eating* economy. If this is unavoidable, then non-decline sustainability cannot be required. This may call for adjusting the latter's demands. For example, it could entail the requirement of using certain resources as little/as late as possible. Indefinite non-decline could not be reachable, though. Should we see here one more reason why the demands of non-decline justice and of non-decline sustainability are not always aligned? Not necessarily. It would rather provide us with a reason to integrate a feasibility proviso in both, as suggested by Barry's quote above.

This points to two last considerations. On the one hand, accepting the idea that sustainability may only be defensible for a limited number of centuries or millennia is slightly less worrying if we insist on the fact that there is *one sense* in which sustainability does not entail a *duty to sustain*. We may be expected to guarantee the *possibility* for the next generation to pursue the human adventure. And we may even hold the view that it would be desirable that the human adventure be pursued. However, if we find it morally *acceptable* for a generation to unanimously decide not to procreate,[25] then there is at least one duty that can be dropped: that of ensuring that a human population will follow ours.

On the other hand, if we accept the view that the history of humankind unavoidably requires some degree of cake-eating, the abyssal question becomes whether there are reasons to prefer a longer and more constrained human history rather than a shorter and less constrained one. And this is an important question for our understanding of both the value of sustainability and the demands of inter-generational justice. We might of course be concerned about how the final generation will fare, especially as its members age and may not benefit from the care of any next gener-ation. However, this will be the case *whatever* the length of human history, whether it ends today or in a millennium or four. The fact that we want some people after us cannot decide the *length* that human history should have. It can at best decide how small we want the last generation to be.

In the end, non-decline sustainability cannot be a necessary requirement of justice whenever we endorse views on justice that allow – or even sometimes require – generational dis-savings. Once we confront non-decline sustainability with non-decline justice, it seems that the possibility of keeping them aligned through integrating the demands identified in this section is much more promising.

Conclusion

In this chapter, I have insisted on significant differences between four different accounts of intergenerational justice.

I connected them with underlying general views about justice. In so doing, I left several things open, including most importantly their metrics. I then proposed ways of reframing these four views in "non-inheritance-ruled" terms. As a third step, I looked at possible definitions of sustainability and engaged in finding out whether sustainability is sufficient and necessary for justice. I identified theories for which it is neither sufficient nor necessary, the latter possibility being the most troubling one. However, since I defined sustainability as non-decline sustainability, it ends up aligning itself relatively well with the non-decline account of intergenerational justice.

This chapter has involved a significant degree of conceptual work. It helps us understand the nature of these views in a deeper manner. I hope to have shown, for instance, the degree to which inheritance-ruled views have very different features from what we are accustomed to in the intragenerational realm. I also indicated the degree to which some views can be reframed in less inheritance-ruled terms. In addition, I insisted on the degree to which what we owe the next generation is hard to fully isolate from what the latter will itself owe its own successors ("their duties are my duties"). And I stressed how difficult it is to provide a definition of sustainability that does not already contain elements from a theory of justice, despite the fact that, at first sight, making sure that something *can* last does not straightforwardly connect with what we *owe* each other.

Beyond conceptual work, I explained why I found the "narrow path" approach most compelling. We would also have to consider the reasons why we may value sustainability. I have pointed to some of the challenges and hope to have shown convincingly at least that the demands of justice and of sustainability do not necessarily converge. Whether one should prevail over the other whenever they diverge is an important question that I will leave open here.

3

What do we owe the future?

When deciding about which world and ways of life to transfer to our successors, we need to make choices, whether we like it or not. Specific preservation or investment options are often mutually incompatible because resources, energy, space, time, brain abilities, patience, or cash are limited. The questions are numerous, intriguing, and significant. Should we preserve heirloom fruit cultivars or concentrate on breeding new ones? Is it wise to grub out centenarian olive trees to replace them with super-intensive groves? Should we sequester carbon in open landscape soils rather than through massive reforestation? Shall we prolong the life of our nuclear power plants or decidedly switch to other energy sources? Is it right if city councils privilege neo-Gothic or art nouveau buildings as protected heritage? Which and how many living languages should we keep alive? Is it better if our children learn classical Greek literature or data science, field geology or the philosophy of privacy law, the art of ceramics or the basics of 3D printing? Do we have to invest more in hospital buildings or in house insulation, in broadening city beltways or in renewing high-speed train tracks? How far should we promote artificial intelligence and the replacement of human tasks by machines? Would it be wrong if we were encouraged to confine our lives more exclusively to virtual reality?[1] Should we render our constitution more difficult to amend, design our waste dumping sites to allow for retrievability, or design our houses to render them less durable? Should we completely open our borders or rather build higher fences and walls?

Our answers will shape the present *and* the future. Admittedly, it is unlikely that philosophical thinking *alone* can provide a full answer to any of these questions. Yet its action-guiding virtues are not necessarily absent. Philosophers can enlighten key elements of method, expose constraints that limit the range of acceptable answers, clear up misunderstandings, or help find out whether the existence of future people makes a difference here. How to identify things worth preserving and how to weigh up alternatives among them? Do some of the options involve basic freedoms that trump the demands of distributive justice? The outcome of this chapter will certainly frustrate anyone who is conscious of the need for urgent action and major changes. Yet there are also limits to how fast an olive tree can grow or to whether a deep understanding of plant physiology *alone* can tell us whether to plant this tree or not. The same holds for philosophy. The world is complex and true turnkey solutions are rare. It does not follow that we should stop planting olive trees, experimenting about plant physiology, or spending a bit of time on becoming more lucid about the philosophical aspects of our actions.

In chapter 1, I looked at *whether* we owe anything to the future as a matter of justice. In chapter 2, I looked at *how much* we owe the future as a matter of justice. In the present chapter, I look at *what* we owe the future as a matter of distributive justice. It is one thing to find out whether we should transfer to the next generation strictly what we inherited, or at least as much, or more, or enough. This only tells us about the *size* of the basket *of some x* that we owe it. Yet it still leaves undefined the nature of this *x*, the *composition* of the stock of "goods" that we should transfer. It tells us about the cake's (share) size without any idea about its ingredients. As we said before, theorists of justice refer to the latter as the "currency" or "metrics" issue ("as much *of what?*," "enough *of what?*" ...). I will begin with setting the basics regarding metrics by concentrating on a simplified setting, allowing those less familiar with theories of justice to grasp what is at stake. I will then move to an intergenerational setting, focusing on three possible proposals. I will pay special attention to preference dynamics and conclude with some thoughts on substitution issues.

Metrics for contemporaries

I begin with a world in which there are no future generations, to set the stage and map the key issues. I aim at completing two tasks. I will show how sufficientarians approach the metrics dimension. I will then illustrate how to go beyond sufficiency, again focusing on the metrics dimension.

Basic needs, basic capabilities
I start with sufficientarianism. We have already touched upon it.[2] It involves defining a threshold. This threshold serves to distinguish what is expected in terms of justice below, above, and across it. Consider an absolute poverty line. You want to know how to handle competing claims among poor people (below the line), competing claims among people who are not poor (above the line), and competing claims between non-poor and poor people (across the line). Sufficientarians primarily care about the last of these, even though they also have things to say about justice among the poor (below the line). They stress the existence of a shift, of a threshold beyond which not only the magnitude but also the nature of our obligations may change. Sufficientarians radically reframe our justice concerns by saying that we should not primarily care about whether some have *less* than others (equality), about whether the condition of the least well-off has been

maximally improved (leximin), about whether *special weight* has been given to the least well-off in maximizing the total of some *x* in society (priority), etc. Rather, we should care about whether all of us have *enough* (sufficiency).

As a result, the non-poor should ensure that no one remains poor. In addition, we should find out how to prioritize claims among the poor, as long as not everyone has been lifted out of poverty. For instance, sufficientarians may expect us either to maximize the number of people reaching the threshold, or to maximally improve the situation of those furthest away from the threshold, or to minimize the average distance from the threshold, etc. In addition, sufficientarians may want to point to non-sufficientarian accounts about justice between the non-poor, the rich, or the super-rich (above the threshold) that are compatible with the sufficientarian view. While they may claim that no further duties of (distributive) justice between the non-poor apply above the threshold, many sufficientarians accept further demands of justice above this threshold. Note as well that within most advanced economies, the ambition in terms of justice generally goes beyond "merely" fighting poverty.

This is the sufficientarian architecture. What about the furniture? We have not said anything yet about the sufficientarian metrics. How is the sufficiency threshold characterized? *What* should people have enough of? Contenders include "basic needs" and "basic capabilities." I am not going to provide here a list of basic needs or basic capabilities.[3] What we rather need to understand here are the reasons underlying the choice of metrics, which also reflects the general motivation for going sufficientarian in the first place. Let me point to two such reasons.

One reason involves the appeal of a more *objective* metrics. Admittedly, even some welfarists endorse a definition of well-being that has an objective dimension, focusing, for example, on pleasure and pain. Yet many welfarists defend a more "preference-based" view, taking note of the fact that different individuals derive very different levels of well-being from the same goods and services. This is so because of people's different tastes and conceptions of what a good life amounts to. Some of us find baroque music essential whereas others consider that listening to a nightingale is magic. The problem of a preference-based account of welfare is that it is quite "subjective," vulnerable to problematic factors that may drive the formation of preferences such as imitation or violence. The sufficientarian bet is that going for something more objective may be compatible with all or most of the conceptions of the good life as long as we don't go beyond a basic threshold. All of us need to eat and breathe, regardless of whether we prefer baroque music, indie folk, or nightingales. Going more "objective" may be easier to operationalize too.

Another reason for going sufficientarian has to do with skepticism about *responsibility*. Egalitarians that are referred to as "luck egalitarians" have proposed incorporating the responsibility dimension within the metrics (equality *of what?*). Instead of aiming at equal welfare, they go for metrics like equal *opportunity for* welfare or equality of "resources" in the sense defined below, allowing for some fair inequalities of welfare remaining. Various paths may lead to stressing responsibility. One may rest on efficiency reasons, assuming that people act more carefully if they are held responsible for some of the consequences of their actions (incentives). One may also stress responsibility out of a sense of fairness, the view that one ought not to impose on others costs associated with certain choices such as getting tattooed or practicing risky sports. In contrast, "basic needs" tends to be a responsibility-insensitive metrics.

A responsibility-sensitive metrics may sound too harsh on those making the wrong choices. It may also be philosophically tricky to isolate the types of choices the costs of which we should pay ourselves, as against those that should lead to redistributive transfers from others. A typical example is whether the coverage by social security of living in a wheelchair should depend on whether it results from a congenital disease, from an accident as a lifeguard, or from an uninsured Formula 1 crash. In short, skepticism about responsibility may lead one to shift to a responsibility-insensitive metrics, which is all the more plausible if we remain below a certain threshold. The relationship between the threshold and responsibility might even be a complex one. For some, the threshold could match the level below which someone is deemed unable to make autonomous choices. Note, however, that one of the main sufficientarian metrics, basic capabilities, is to some degree responsibility-sensitive, through the way it articulates "basic capabilities" and "functionings." And note as well that in many countries, as a matter of actual policy, basic income support often requires the willingness to work.

Dworkinian resourcism

I have stressed two common features of a sufficientarian metrics: its attempts at leaving less room for preferences and for responsibility. In addition, it often takes the pluralistic form of a list (e.g. of basic needs) rather than that of a single umbrella currency (like "real freedom" or "welfare"). We will need to assess the relevance (if any) of these features to intergenerational relations. Before that, my second task is to give a sense of what may be required above the sufficiency threshold. By way of illustration, consider Ronald Dworkin's account of what he calls equality *of resources*. This is one of the possible approaches to characterizing the demands of justice above the threshold. And I take it to be one of the most plausible. Here, I don't focus so much on equality as such (the principle) but rather on what "resources" mean (the metrics). The latter should not be understood in a simplistic manner as "each of us should have the same amount of cash" or "each of us should have the same initial access to natural resources." Rather, Dworkin's approach consists in proposing decision procedures. Let me present them and highlight their underlying rationale.[4]

Roughly, in Dworkin's world, people have talents (internal resources) and tastes (preferences), and they are surrounded by scarce external goods (fertile land, inherited road infrastructure, etc.). The first step in Dworkin's procedure involves a *hypothetical and equalitarian auction* for *external* goods. Each of us is granted equal purchasing power. We express our tastes through bidding for external resources. The degree to which our preferences will be satisfied depends on what the preferences of others will be. If I am the only person interested in a plot of land, my preferences may be fully satisfied. On the contrary, if others are also keen on it, my access to it will have to reflect the degree to which acquiring it would deprive others from satisfying their own preferences.

What we observe with such a procedure is that equality in purchasing-power levels may translate into very *unequal* levels of welfare in the end. The latter inequalities are fair under Dworkin's account, though. And these inequalities will not necessarily reflect responsibility in the full sense. Rather, they will reflect not only what resources happen to be available but also how much satisfying my preferences would cost others. That will also depend on whether the good at stake is rival or not, on whether economies of scale obtain, etc.

Hence, Dworkin wants to use the idea of an auction or a market and its ability to track information about what and how much others want of certain goods, albeit hypothetically. This means that if people want to know whether their consumption level is fair, they need a good sense of what goods are actually available as well as "information about the actual cost their choices impose on other people."[5] This requires knowledge about the content, intensity, frequency, and distribution of their preferences.

There are several other steps in Dworkin's approach. Besides a hypothetical auction for external resources, he envisages a hypothetical insurance against handicaps, again involving people having equal initial purchasing power. This is meant to reflect the differential importance that people will attach to being deaf, blind, dyslexic, etc. The idea is to compensate for some differences in internal resources (those resulting from "brute luck") while not doing so for others (those resulting from "option luck").

So, basically, what Dworkin is offering us is an egalitarian account of justice that allows for some inequalities to develop, and hypothetical procedures to both understand this account and pave the way for real-life institutions that could approximate them, including possibly through cautiously extracting information from actual market prices or through modifying insurance rules.

Guessing future talents and tastes

I have just presented one possible account of distributive justice for contemporaries. It combines a sufficientarian basis with equality of resources above the threshold. This is of course only one among the possible combinations. What matters here is to point to the challenges faced by the metrics of this account when transposed to the intergenerational sphere. I begin by taking future tastes (preferences) as given (or exogenous). I will relax this assumption in the next section. At this stage, let me stress that some of the challenges will only affect relations between non-overlapping generations, whereas others also apply to coexisting generations. Hence, it will be worth keeping in mind the "overlap/non-overlap" dimension again to grasp the scope of the problems at stake. Unsurprisingly, they are more serious for non-overlapping generations. Relatedly, we may try to get around the latter problems through relying on duties between *overlapping* generations, linking ourselves to the more remote future in a stepwise manner, through a succession of overlaps. This stepwise approach commends itself for a variety of reasons. Actual coexistence allows for actual coordination and deliberation. Temporal proximity reduces uncertainties, because, among other reasons, transfers of resources toward the remote future depend on the willingness of "transit" generations to effectively take part in the transfer effort.

What happens when we apply equality of resources to *non-overlapping* generations? I begin with "talents" (internal resources). A generation whose bundle of talents is less advantageous may be owed compensation. While backward compensation beyond the overlap is not feasible, forward compensation is. Internal resources will not necessarily remain constant over time. We may try and predict the evolution of some talents. For instance, as IQ seems to be stagnating in many societies, it might possibly go down in the future.[6] New physical disabilities may emerge, for example triggered by new viruses. The average level of internal resources in future generations depends on a variety of factors, some of which are inherited from previous generations: teratogenic pollutants accumulated in our landscapes, the medical technologies to fix disabilities and to "enhance" us, skills promoted or neglected by the educational choices of our parents, etc. Hence, the makeup of future internal resources depends in part on the past. Even if it does not, it may require intergenerational compensation as long as differences do not result from the disadvantaged generation's own costly choices.

The problem goes beyond "merely" predicting what level of talent, skills, and abilities future generations will enjoy, and how the evolution of technology will render some of them pointless while others will become crucial in their societies. The difficulty also has to do with obtaining information about future *preferences*. Remember that Dworkin stressed the need to assess people's bundle of internal resources through the prism of their own preferences and of the opportunity cost for the preference satisfaction of others. There might be no problem if less talented generations don't consider themselves disadvantaged at all.

Yet two difficulties arise with respect to future *prefer-ences*. The first, to which I return in the next section, is that the formation of future people's preferences will signifi-cantly be influenced by their predecessors. The second is that future people currently have no preferences. It is essential for a Dworkinian to come up with some sort of *information exchange* device, through which a generation can learn about another generation's preference set, even if it is not done through price revelation based on an insurance mechanism in the case of internal resources. However, when generations don't overlap, even the roughest proxies of such mechanisms are simply unavailable. Future people will of course be able to tell later whether their level of preference satisfaction is higher than our own, with the help of future historians. And we can of course also try and guess what their future skills and abilities are likely to be, how technology will interact with them, and how far this is likely to both shape and satisfy their preferences. But the key thing is that this is going to be very rough. No actual exchange of information is possible.

So we ought to keep in mind the fact that preferences matter and that differences in preferences are likely. However, we can at best take a relatively wild guess at these future preferences, especially for remote generations. In fact, the same also arises with respect to "external" resources: our built heritage, our biodiversity, and the state of our aquifers, as well as the available technology at some point in the future. This adds further uncertainty, as material and immaterial objects should be approached through the prism of current and future preferences. The value of a barrel of oil will depend on the future state of our technology and on the energy choices embodied in the society that the future will inherit. But this value of a barrel of oil will also depend on future people's own preferences.

What to conclude? First, for *overlapping* generations, a "resourcist" perspective à la Dworkin can still hold and translate into forms of real exchange of information. This will tell us how respective bundles of external and internal resources are evaluated by the respective generations at hand. For "resourcists," such an exchange matters not only out of concerns of democratic legitimacy, but also more directly to implement a theory of justice. Second, for generations that do *not* overlap, neither a synchronic exchange of information, nor any approximation of it, is possible. Yet we can still try and predict elements of the future, including the likely content of future preferences. And even if the picture becomes increasingly blurred as we look further into the future, we should at least take into account in our decisions that future preferences *may differ* significantly from ours. Third, I have not discussed the sufficientarian metrics here. This is because sufficientarians do not need to know about future preferences. Yet they still need to anticipate the future state of talents, technologies, natural resources, etc. in order to know what will be necessary to cover basic needs or basic capabilities in the future.

Hence, the possibility of implementing policies inspired by equality of resources beyond the overlap is not ruled out. In addition, even sufficientarians, while not concerned about future preferences as such, also face prediction challenges. Given such uncertainties, we may have to accept less precision than equality of resources would normally command among contemporaries. With one important caveat: as we have said, the remote future can be approached through the close future. Being fair toward the generations with which we overlap may help us project ourselves almost a century ahead, given the life expectancy of some of our youngest contemporaries. This may be a way of implementing both sufficiency and equality of resources intergenerationally, reaching the remote future in a stepwise manner. We pass the baton to our direct successors and allow them to readjust their policies according to what they anticipate their own future will look like. Generations pass each other a basket of goods and trust the eyes of their direct descendants to see beyond their own horizon.

Taking preference dynamics seriously: three proposals

So far, I have left aside the issue of taste or preference *formation*. In fact, among contemporaries as well, our preferences and practices inform the preferences of others, in various ways. In market or insurance schemes too, learning about the preferences of others may lead to adjusting not only the degree to which we expect our preferences to be met, but also the content of these very preferences. Yet, while preference adjustments take place all throughout our lives, they tend to be especially intense at the early stages of life. This is the reason why the intergenerational dimension is key. The direction that the next generation's preferences will take depends very much on the ways of life and the world that the generation is *exposed* to as well as on the *education* we provide for it.

In addition, whether future preferences will be satisfied can be approached from both ends. We can ensure that the world we bequeath to our children is up to the level they are likely to expect. Alternatively, we can make sure that their expectations remain limited or very flexible, and hence easy to satisfy. We return below to whether these two avenues are equally desirable. This is an important issue. For what is the point of patiently defending a principle of justice – as we did in the previous chapter – if in the end its demands beyond sufficiency can easily be met by engineering the preferences of future people, regardless of how much "stuff" we transfer to them? I will now explore a few possible substantive principles that touch on the dynamics of future preferences and may help us address this challenge. Note that the challenge affects relations between *both* non-overlapping and overlapping generations.

One component consists in defining a thin conception of the good life and what it would require, referring to some of the polyvalent resources likely to be of significant use to all humans, irrespective of their specific conception of what matters in life.[7] Soils, education systems, and political regimes are needed to implement most views of the good life. And a series of concepts – such as the notion of "critical natural capital"[8] – is usually referred to in such a spirit. Here, note that this "common base" idea can be viewed from a liberal angle in general – what is needed for any conception of the good life to flourish – or from its sufficientarian version in particular – the resources needed for anyone to have a *sufficiently* good life. Of course, the degree to which the demands of sufficiency are met will influence the content of future preference sets. Yet this as such does not tell us about the types of preferences we should inculcate through education. We will return to this.

Proposal 1: intangible heritage
Consider a first possible proposal. Choices in energy systems, transportation infrastructure, farmland practices, blue-sky research priorities, linguistic policy, religious doctrine, institutional design, etc. will *bind* generations ahead. The need for "transition pathways" confirms the pervasiveness of path dependencies that render overnight changes impossible and reversion costly. Our dependence on fossil fuels offers a sad illustration. Such path dependencies may lead to a mismatch with future preferences, while also influencing the content of such future preferences. Our question: is it *possible* and *desirable* to render our choices *less* binding on future people?[9]

One possible modality could consist in putting a stronger emphasis on *intangible* heritage in our ways of life. However, while shifting to intangible heritage may not require as many hands for its preservation, it will require at least as many brains. Moving from *in situ* seeds conservation to a seed vault, replacing buildings with building manuals, or abandoning libraries to replace them with oral traditions all require massive educational efforts to keep these assets constantly alive, to put libraries back into our brains. Hence, even dematerializing and "going intangible" will still entail significant path dependencies since intangible heritage preservation remains time-, brain-, and labor-intensive. It even requires a significant material basis in many cases. Going down that avenue will thus certainly also remain binding for the future.

Two additional dimensions should be kept in mind, one about respecting existing preferences, the other about efficiency. Regarding the former, an exclusive focus on intangible resources would clash with the conceptions of those within the *current* generation who value non-ephemeral physical environments and the way in which humans *physically* interact with the world and between each other. As a result, a liberal approach to intergenerational justice will have to leave some room for at least some long-term projects that materialize through long-term material objects (bridges, old monuments, nature reserves, original paintings from old masters, etc.) as a way of respecting the views of those among *current* people who emphasize materialized transfers.

Moreover, given our embodied lives and the material needs they entail (food, shelter, mobility, etc.), aiming at leaving less physical trace raises serious *efficiency* concerns. Efforts at increasing the fertility and water-harvesting capacity of our soils, investments to build durable infrastructures to transport goods and people or to produce (renewable) energy, or work done to renovate old houses would be lost. Our material heritage tremendously increases the well-being of our societies. In a scenario in which, while having inherited all the necessary knowledge, we would need to rebuild from scratch, again and again, all the infrastructure accumulated over generations to allow our society to function, the loss would be major. Most theories of justice care about efficiency in one way or another, especially when they don't stick to a strict principle of equality. Efficiency is of course relevant to reaching sufficiency. We see below why "resourcists" à la Dworkin should also not be indifferent to efficiency gains.

The takeaway message about this "hands-off," "intangible-heritage-focused" strategy is that constraining the future seems unavoidable, even if we go for more dematerialized forms of generational bequests. In addition, leaving no physical trace at all is also undesirable, especially for efficiency reasons. This being said, going *more* intangible may be part of the desired strategy, as will be discussed below (proposal 3). Also, since exposure to the world as we inherit it will affect the preferences that future people will form, we ought to pursue our thinking about which substantive constraints (if any) may be added to take seriously the *dynamic* dimension of preference formation and the challenge we formulated above.

Proposal 2: open options

Can we come up with an additional substantive proposal? There is an "open options" idea both in future-generations literature ("keeping options open") and in the philosophy of education (a "child's right to an open future").[10] It stresses that alternatives ought to exist, which points to an idea of *diversity* in ways of life. And these alternatives need to be open. They should be more than *formally* accessible, more than merely possible "in books." Yet can we be more specific than this?

What seems central is a *liberal* requirement about preference formation, the fact of valuing the possibility for people to make up and to *change* their mind about what is essential in their life, for instance as a result of critical introspection or of exchanging reasons with others through deliberation. In a sense, in the intergenerational literature as well as in the philosophy of education, the idea of "open options" seems both to acknowledge the path-dependency in which we are caught (something we may need to opt out from) and to stress the need to allow for deviations (availability of something we can opt into).

Future preferences don't emerge in a vacuum. They feed to a significant extent on exposure and experience, which is key for the "openness" dimension of "options open."[11]

A child is unlikely to form a strong preference for playing music today or in the future unless it is significantly exposed to music, be it through receiving music lessons or through watching and listening to her peers playing. I am not even referring here to complex age-specific mechanisms associated with early brain exposure to the sounds of other languages or with values establishment through the political socialization of teenagers. I am merely saying that current and future generations are unlikely to give much importance to birding if there are neither birds nor active birdwatchers around.[12] If we care about *real* freedom or autonomy in forming different preferences and about the importance of exposure, we need to ensure that diverse communities embodying different *ways of life* coexist in our societies *today*. This is valuable for the current generation and our ability to change preferences. It is also valuable for future generations for the same reasons. And it may be a challenging position to adopt if we consider the possibility of a uniform world in which all of us would have ended up freely choosing a single way of life within a generation.

Does this requirement of preserving a diversity *of ways of life* tell us anything about the need to preserve things like *biodiversity* or *linguistic diversity*? The connection is not straightforward. For being confronted with other ways of life also means being confronted with people for whom biodiversity only matters for its services to agriculture, with Zen dry garden fans who value hyper-simplified environments leading to meditation, with activists promoting a monolingual world with no further obstacles to peaceful global communication, or with those who fear cultural diversity as a threat to solidarity. Hence, defenses of extensive biodiversity preservation and of rich multilingualism will not necessarily find full support in the need to keep options open. This does not mean that we cannot come up with *independent* arguments. It merely means that they probably cannot flow only from stressing the need for preserving a diversity *of ways of life*.

I would also submit that arguments for preserving biodiversity or linguistic diversity should rest not merely on their virtues *for the future* but rather also on accounts of why they seem valuable to *us*, and to some extent *for* us. Such accounts may of course entail, as a significant "side effect," that they be valuable for the future too, justifying their preservation.

In fact, what I have just said for biodiversity and linguistic diversity also holds for putting flesh on the demands of "open options" more generally. Let us assume that current preferences, the values we endorse, are *sufficiently diverse* – a plausible assumption at the global level.[13] We can build on the content and diversity of *existing* preferences. And one advantage is that most people's conception of the good life *includes* valuing the preservation *into the future* of their preferred way of life. Current people may value the spirit of beekeeping or the atmosphere of jazz clubs, the mysteries of poetry or the mind-absorbing nature of solitary knitting, the adrenaline of the marketplace or the disinterested nature of the non-profit sector, the freedom of urban anonymity or the stimulating nature of a multicultural environment. When they do, it often matters to them that the next generation gets a chance to experience it too.

Let me take stock. I insisted on the idea of a common sufficientarian basis. Beyond it, I argued that the hands-off, "intangible-heritage" approach is insufficient. I then tried to put flesh on the "open options" requirement. The need to guarantee a diversity of valuable options alive derives from both the importance for liberals of enabling preference *change* and the importance of actual exposure for preference *formation*. The proposed approach provides us with an idea of *which* ways of life to preserve for the future, assuming that something valuable for the present has some chances of being valuable for the future. In addition, preserving such ways of life into the future usually also matters to present people. Note two rules of thumb, then, derived from the current distribution of options. First, when the present values something, the future is likely to value it. Second, when the present values something, the present is likely to value its continuation into the future.[14]

Of course, this strategy that builds on present diversity in ways of life has limitations and leaves many questions open. It is unclear to what extent fully secularized societies might have to preserve *some* active churches, or completely urbanized societies large bits of countryside, in order to keep options open notwithstanding the current distribution of preferences. Also, new valuable ways of life keep popping up, some of which are hard to anticipate. Conversely, it might be that some ways of life be gradually eliminated through a transgenerational "learning from experience" process. If so, does it not follow that transferring gradually fewer options over time would be acceptable? Above, I didn't discuss more broadly the role here of constitutional essentials that constrain the range of acceptable ways of life, for instance on grounds of their compatibility with basic liberties. Nor did I have space to discuss the degree to which one should expect the next generations to stick to the same constitutional essentials, including non-procedural ones, which can be rendered more likely through forms of constitutional rigidity.[15] These are crucial dimensions too, of course.

Proposal 3: inculcating frugal preferences

My account of the "open options" requirement linked it to preference dynamics. The latter involves exposure to ways of life, including at an early age, but also learning through formal education. The question is whether we should not only preserve the conditions for a diverse set of open options, but also privilege, within this set of options, those that are "cheaper." In a world in which exposure to resource-intensive ways of life tends to feed increasingly expensive preferences, a move toward cheaper preferences can come from the anticipation of having fewer resources in the future or from a concern for leaving enough resources to the future. Note a tension: while our current ways of life may encourage expensive preferences, concerns about what will be left in the future or about what we should do for it may operate in the opposite direction. A vehicle other than exposure to current ways of life may thus be needed to convey the latter concerns. Education could be such a vehicle.

How to define a "cheap" or "expensive" taste or preference from within a theory of justice? "Cheap" can mean both "less resource-intensive" (low-expense) and "less valuable" (low-worth), the latter being rather pejorative. However, "expensive" refers here to preferences whose satisfaction is resource-intensive, time-intensive, labor-intensive, carbon-intensive, etc. in a specific way. What matters is the costs that their satisfaction imposes on *others*. Developing fine grafting skills or mastering the whistling language Silbo Gomero may take a lot of time and effort. One could even be under the impression that the activities that one most values actually tend to be the costliest. And yet they will not necessarily qualify as costly in the present sense, for they might entail no significant (opportunity) cost *for others*. Certain goals may be labor-intensive to pursue *for ourselves*, while not necessarily burdening others. Admittedly, whether they impose costs on others depends on the initial ownership status of the world and on what we owe others, too. If we stress our positive duties toward others, even time-consuming hobbies that use no material resources would impose costs on others, including future people.

Hereinafter, I will take "cheap," "inexpensive," and "frugal" as synonyms. Let me give two examples of ways in which we impose costs on other generations. First, a *front-loaded good* situation occurs whenever the distribution of burdens and benefits of an activity is such that benefits are concentrated in the present and burdens in the future.[16] Nuclear energy and nuclear waste are a case in point. We enjoy energy use now and leave the waste management to the future. I am not saying that there are no benefits for the future, for instance if energy is used to develop new sustainable technologies, to build passive houses, or to redesign agricultural landscapes to render them more climate-resilient. I am simply saying that the distribution of burdens and benefits will still be very unequal across time. This is the temporal equivalent of a hypothetical world with two equally endowed auctioneers and two plots of land for sale, in which one auctioneer has more *land-intensive* preferences than the other. She would need not only to buy one plot, but also to purchase the right to drop her waste on the other person's land, or to buy some of the second plot too. Front-loaded goods illustrate one way in which preferences can be expensive for others. Rather than being more land-intensive in a strict sense, they are time-intensive, i.e. they entail occupying people's minds, hands, and land for a longer time than our own period of existence, because our successors will have to continue dealing with them.

The other example involves *rising expectations.*[17] When a new generation tends to have higher expectations than the previous one, satisfying these preferences will be more labor- or resource-intensive, unless the rise in expectations strictly follows some (exogenous) rise in technological productivity. Rising expectations can be compared again to a situation in which one auctioneer needs more land than the other to reach the same level of satisfaction. While in the nuclear waste example, it is the earlier generation that has expensive preferences, in the rising standard one, it is the later one that does. Note that if the rising trend continues, each generation will have preferences more expensive than those of its predecessor while being cheaper than those of its successor.

In a way, the rising standards case is also *similar* to the nuclear waste one. If our children happen to form preferences that involve a higher standard of living, we may be willing to put in extra effort to help our children reach such a standard. It does not mean that this is the parents' duty, at least not within a resourcist framework. Of course, rising standards are a problem if they lead the new generation to deprive the poorest members of the previous one, with which it coexists, of significant means of existence. Yet whenever the higher standard is also an *unsustainable* one, for example due to its non-renewable natural resources base, the problem is that it imposes costs on future people, as in the nuclear waste case.

Hence, resourcists may want to object to rising standards in two ways. They will refuse to impose extra burdens on predecessors to satisfy their successors' *more* resource-intensive preferences. The *rise* is key here. And they will deny the right to act upon such preferences whenever they are *too* resource-intensive, to avoid depriving successors of the resources they would be able to purchase in a hypothetical, cross-generational auction. Here, it is the standard's *height* rather than its *rise* that is key. In short, resourcists will object to rising standards if they impose burdens on other generations, notably if eco-economic decoupling can only be achieved to a limited degree, rendering these standards unsustainable.

Let me now assume here that school-based education has *some* impact on people's preferences.[18] The issue of frugal preferences raises at least the following questions:

Q1: *May* we teach frugal preferences to our children?
Q2: *Should* we teach frugal preferences to our children?
Q3: Is it preferable to acquire frugal preferences through education rather than through exposure to a deteriorating heritage?
Q4: Does teaching frugal preferences allow us to let our heritage deteriorate further?

While I cannot go in depth into each of these questions, let me say a few things about each of them. Q1 is about whether it could be wrong to teach frugal tastes to our children. Liberals would certainly not object to some social groups engaging in a frugal lifestyle, including exposing their children to it and teaching it to them.[19] The formal school system could also confront children with the idea of frugality and explore its implications with them.

Q2 goes one step further. Here, it is not about what's wrong with teaching frugality. Rather it is about what's wrong with *not* teaching frugality. Is it preferable or even required that our generation teaches frugality to the next one? Teaching frugality to individuals will not only allow them to reach higher levels of preference satisfaction for themselves with fewer material resources. It will also free up more material resources for others to do the same. This matters in a context of overconsumption and massive global injustice. Teaching frugality can contribute to a happier and more just global society, enabling individuals to be more efficient at transforming scarce material resources into well-being, and reducing the latter's scarcity.[20]

Also, teaching frugality will enable individuals to be *freer in forming new preferences*, because having less resource-intensive preferences makes it easier to switch preferences and adjust to what we believe to be the most valuable options.[21] While we are admittedly considering costs for ourselves rather than for others here, in a society of interdependent people and with a strong degree of division of labor, the two are interconnected. Admittedly, Dworkinian "resourcists" do not *require* equal levels of preference *satisfaction*. However, it does not follow that they ought to remain indifferent to the degree to which preferences can be satisfied, and to the degree to which people can freely form and change preferences.[22] Our answer to Q2 is, then, that while we ought not necessarily *impose* frugal preferences on all, we *should* certainly confront the next generation with them as a possible way of life, not only through the school system, but even as parents, arguably as a duty of *justice*.[23]

About Q3, teaching frugality is preferable to inducing frugality through resource deprivation. For it better preserves future freedom in forming different preferences, even if levels of preference satisfaction currently look the same under both scenarios.

As to Q4, if we were sure that the next generation were to form preferences that are cheaper than ours, due to exogenous factors, would it not be acceptable to transfer to them a lesser stock of resources than we inherited? Wouldn't they still be able to reach the same level of preference satisfaction as us? And would transferring a lesser stock not even be *required* in such a case, out of concern for the conservation costs to the present, in the spirit of what we stressed in the previous chapter as a ground for defending the "narrow path" view?

The problem is that this would lead to people with expensive preferences receiving more resources than people with cheap preferences. This would go against the resourcist egalitarian ideal that equalizes initial "purchasing powers" rather than welfare levels. Adjusting resources to the demandingness of preferences would unequally distribute the real freedom to form one's own preferences. It is one thing to endorse a frugal life because this is our *only* option; it is another to voluntarily endorse it while having enough resources to adopt non-frugal preferences too. So the best mix for the generations ahead is one in which we inherit an "objectively" rich world and in which we tend to form cheap preferences. We increase our ability to satisfy our preferences, increase the chances that they are freely formed, reduce the cost of changing them if needed, and reduce the costs that they impose on others. None of this presupposes the claim – rejected by resourcists – that preferences should necessarily be equally satisfied.

The challenge is to make sure that the fact of transferring a rich basket of resources does not simultaneously lead the next generation to adopt *expensive* preferences. Hence, keeping in mind the dynamics of exposure to our current ways of life *and* to the education that we provide to the next generation is crucial. We ought to *cultivate a gap* between the world as it is in terms of resources and the aspirations we form, a gap that would be threatened if preferences fully adjusted to exposure rather than to education. To some extent, education can sometimes act as a counterpower to exposure. We need to constantly keep in mind the role of education as confronting us with alternative ways of life able to preserve this gap between the resources that we could use and the resources we need to support our way of life.

Hence, there is at least a *pro tanto* case for promoting cheaper preferences for the next generation, for the reasons presented above. And promoting frugality may be achieved through education, but also through leading frugal lives ourselves, even if it does not turn out to be the dominant way of life.[24] Of course, there is complexity: promoting more frugal preferences may enter into tension with the idea of preserving a *diversity* of ways of life; it may merely slow down resource exhaustion rather than fix it; it could sometimes turn out to be counterproductive, through reducing pressure toward precious technological innovation. While an all-things-considered assessment ought to take such considerations into account, there are good prima facie reasons to promote frugality.

Substitutions

Hence, we can expect each generation to encourage the next generation to adopt frugal preferences, which may be achieved through education, but also through leading more frugal lives ourselves.[25] Note that what I said holds for "resourcist" egalitarians. Does it also hold for sufficientarians? It does, since going for less resource-intensive preferences increases the probability of reaching sufficiency for all. Yet, above sufficiency, this still does not provide us with much indication about the absolute *level* at which the resource-intensity of our preferences should be set. It also gives us only incomplete information about the *composition* of the basket of goods to be transferred to the next generations. Rather than adding further proposals to the three that I explored, I will stress here, before concluding, how our metrics translate into *substitution* issues. We can formulate the following questions:

Is it acceptable to substitute ...

... resources with cheap preferences?
... external resources with internal ones?
... material resources with technology?
... natural resources with artificial ones?

Let me say a few words about each of these questions. On "resources vs. preferences," I have just discussed whether we can compensate a loss in material resources with less demanding preferences, namely with an increase in the "conversion rate" of preferences, an improvement of their ability to convert resources into well-being. I concluded in the negative from a "resourcist" perspective (in the Dworkinian sense).

On "external vs. internal resources," the idea would be to compensate a degradation of material resources with an enhancement of internal resources. We would improve the capacity of our minds and bodies to face more intense heat waves, a more polluted environment, more frequent pandemics, more complex decisions, etc. Note that the issue is not whether, if the degradation of material resources becomes unavoidable, we should improve people's internal resources. The issue is whether we may contemplate letting our material stocks shrink once our internal resources have been enhanced. In a sense, the intuition is in line with the "resources vs. preferences" issue, robust bodies and minds replacing frugal preferences in this case. Consider the two alternatives: "harsh climate and robust bodies and minds" vs. "mild climate and weaker bodies and minds." Can't they be equivalent?

There is no ready-made answer to how far, for instance, climate mitigation can be substituted with adapting our physiology to a harsher environment. The "resourcist" approach is not necessarily very explicit about how to trade losses in external resources against gains in talents. Arguments will probably have to be elaborated independently, building on e.g. objections to or cases for physical enhancement in the philosophical literature.

As to "material resources vs. technology," it is a central concern for the "weak" vs. "strong" sustainability debate.[26] We can make at least four plausible claims here. First, prohibiting the consumption of resources if they are non-renewable in the name of future generations would be a problem. It would entail that no generation could ever consume them. Some consumption of non-renewable resources should be defensible, the whole issue being under which conditions. Second, caring about an increase in material resources while forgetting to transfer the technology would be very problematic too. A lot is lost, for instance, if we go for a preservation *in situ* of plant cultivars without keeping alive the memory of how these plants can be used. More generally, differences in wealth across countries don't primarily reflect differences in material resources, which suggests that knowledge and technology play a very significant role in wealth building – leaving aside "Dutch disease" issues. Third, it is doubtful that technology can proceed without a significant material basis, which means that we should be careful in allowing for substitution at this level. Fourth, and relatedly, it may sometimes be harder to keep technologies alive than to conserve material heritage, the latter often being able to survive over time without active interventions on our part.

In the end, going for a strong sustainability requirement, hence for strong limits on the substitutability of material resources with cultural ones, needs to rest on specific arguments. Such arguments can point to uncertainties about future preferences and uses, to the freedom of future people to develop different technologies, to efficiency concerns about the likelihood of more productive future technologies, to claims of differential ownership status of material and intangible resources within what we inherited, or to claims about the value of material resources for beings other than humans.

Finally, the "natural vs. artificial" issue is a notoriously difficult one. Ideally, we should be able to say something about proposals such as E. O. Wilson's "Half-Earth,"[27] the latter calling for preserving half of the Earth's surface as habitat for wild species. We should also be able to tell whether there are reasons of justice to object to moving our planet to an artificial dome, one full of biologically very diverse species, all genetically transformed by human intervention.[28] Of course, we will need arguments for why and how far "wilderness" is valuable. Such arguments may be anthropocentric or not, instrumental or not. We also need to understand the connection between wilderness and physical heritage, as the genetic *information* of wild species may be part of our natural heritage too.

Does a "resourcist" framework have anything *specific* to say about this "artificialization" concern? I doubt it. Of course, it will be sensitive to the place of natural environments and wilderness in people's *current* preference sets. Yet it is perfectly conceivable to add to a human-focused resourcist approach further demands of justice toward other living beings, including non-domesticated ones, that may take a less resourcist shape. This can lead to a variety of duties to animals, for instance, such as great apes, and may of course include future members of such non-human species. The fact that resourcism may not have much to say about it does not need to mean that it ought to be treated as an irrelevant set of considerations. Hence, working out our duties to future wild animals, including duties of justice enforceable by the state, is one of the ways in which we may feed a broader sense of what we owe the future, independently of the current state of our conceptions of the good life.

Conclusion

My goal has been to explore how the metrics of a theory of justice could apply to an intergenerational setting. We are talking about what we owe each other as a matter of justice here, not as a matter of general morality. As a result, richer value systems could operate when it comes to defining our ethical duties, including within family lines. As far as justice is concerned, i.e. duties that we could impose on citizens, I began with a dual view mixing a sufficientarian basis and an egalitarian component above sufficiency. This was meant to stress that the metrics of the sufficientarian basis differs from that of the egalitarian component above sufficiency. In fact, the sufficientarian metrics (basic needs, basic capabilities) does not raise specific problems, with a twofold caveat. Finding out whether the requirements of this metrics are met will need at least some degree of prediction about future talents, technologies, and resources. In addition, teaching frugal tastes may also serve the goal of intergenerational sufficientarianism.

As far as implementing Dworkinian "resourcism" is concerned, I considered first our duties of prediction in a static preferences context. I then looked at preference dynamics. Besides going a little bit more intangible and besides the importance of "open options" (including from the angle of preference dynamics), I discussed extensively whether justice commands a duty to teach frugality to our children. We may have a moral duty to do so, and justice – be it resourcist egalitarian or even sufficientarian – may be served by it. However, it remains unclear whether it can be seen as an enforceable duty of justice as such. The dynamics of preferences is central – even though not unique – to the intergenerational context. It has implications for duties not only between non-overlapping generations but also between overlapping ones. And note that it points to a potential tension between exposure to certain ways of life and what education ought to stress about the implications of such ways of life, which renders education programs all the more important.

It is a notoriously difficult task to translate the metrics of a theory of justice into actual policy. And it is probably even harder to do so in an intergenerational context, as the discussion on substitutions also illustrates. For we face special challenges regarding the possibility of information exchange about preferences, as well as regarding preference formation. Going through the intermediary of overlapping generations seems crucial, as the latter context allows for actual exchanges of information about preferences. Yet this remains an imperfect solution, as it still means that a few generations will share their view, leaving all the other future generations out of the picture. This information deficit may of course render the metrics of sufficientarianism tempting, as the latter is less preference dependent. Yet limiting ourselves to a sufficientarian basis seems to excessively limit the demands of justice, and we have shown that even sufficientarians will need to predict the future.

This conclusion may be disappointing, especially to those insisting on the careful definition of a *principle* of intergenerational justice as proposed in the previous chapter, or to those who, in light of the serious limitations faced by intergenerational decision-making discussed below in chapter 5, insist on the need to fall back on robust and substantive approaches of what we owe the future as a matter of *justice*. Yet, while it is not much, it gives us at least some direction as to where to go. And it gives us a sense of where further research is needed.

4

What are our *climate duties* to the future?

I have stressed the possibility of obligations of justice toward non-overlapping generations, the variety of possible principles with their respective properties, and the challenges associated with metrics of justice in an intergenerational context. Here, I will look – by way of illustration – into one of the central policy issues of our times and at its intergenerational dimension: climate justice. Global warming is cross-generational. The temperature increase that we are experiencing results to a large extent from greenhouse gas emissions that have been accumulating since at least the mid-nineteenth century. The inertia of climate change is such that it would survive us even if we were on the right mitigation tracks today. There is a range of the issues raised by global warming that have to do with intergenerational *justice*.

Before I proceed, let me remind the reader about two dimensions stressed in the introduction that are relevant to the present chapter. First, I will focus on generations as birth cohorts, even though issues of justice between age groups also arise in the case of climate change, for instance when considering the effects of heat waves on the elderly. Second, I am not assuming here that issues of intergenerational justice trump issues of global or gender justice, for instance, in the climate case. Besides acknowledging that intergenerational justice issues interact with issues in these other dimensions of justice,[1] I am merely assuming here that the intergenerational dimension is significant for climate justice and that the latter is a significant domain for intergenerational justice.

Past harms, non-overlap, and special obligations

Historical emissions of greenhouse gas are a *fact* with present consequences. Past emissions exhibit three features that are central to a climate-justice-focused account. First, levels of historical emissions *differ* across countries. Some countries contributed much more in the past to the problems faced today and tomorrow. Second, the *knowledge* that people had in the past about the global warming potential of their emissions and its significance differed from ours. Physical chemist Svante Arrhenius admittedly knew about the greenhouse effect as far back as the end of the nineteenth century. Yet he rather saw it as good news, as he was fearing a new ice age. What matters is what people in the past *should* have known. Arguably, our ignorance as a society was not objectionable until the second half of the twentieth century, perhaps even up to 1990 – the year of the first Intergovernmental Panel on Climate Change (IPCC) assessment report.[2] Third, part of these emissions were caused by generations that are now *dead*. When referring to pre-1990 emissions of CO_2, the two former features are present while the third is partly so. A significant part of today's population can still be regarded as *causally* responsible for some of the pre-1990 greenhouse gas emissions. And yet the third feature is key too.

To sum up, pre-1990 emission levels were not uniform across countries (differentiated past emissions); epistemic expectations toward past decision-makers differ from those we have toward today's leaders (excusable past ignorance); and most of those causally responsible for past

emissions are not alive anymore (non-overlap). If we want
to reject the conclusions below, I assume that we need to
drop one of these assumptions. They are worth keeping in
mind, especially because claims about historical emissions
very often tend to be framed in rectificatory terms – namely
as duties of certain groups to compensate *harms* suffered
by other groups due to such past emissions. I discussed in
chapter 1 a central difficulty faced by transgenerational
harm-based views, and I will now show that it is not the
only one.

Let me, then, formulate two key *intergenerational*
questions raised by historical emissions:

Q1: Are there *special* obligations of current (and future)
    members of group A toward current (and future)
    members of group B due to higher per capita pre-1990
    emissions by group A (than those of groups B or C) and/
    or to greater harms from pre-1990 emissions suffered by
    current (or future) members of group B (than by those
    of groups A or C)?
Q2: Do members of the current generation have *special*
    obligations toward members of future generations
    because of pre-1990 emissions?

Q1 focuses on the duties of specific groups toward
members of other groups, including future ones. In
contrast, Q2 deals with the duties of the current generation, taken as a whole, toward the future. I will devote
most of this section to Q1, returning at the end to Q2.
Now, to answer Q1, one should see that the historical-
emissions problem exhibits parallels with and differences
from the standard historical injustice of genocide or
slavery. This is worth stressing because public discourse
tends to approach historical emissions in rectificatory
terms, grounding duties on a (wrongful-)harm diagnosis.
While this comparison will take us a few paragraphs,
it will clarify assumptions that are too often hidden
in the historical-emissions debate. Consider claims for

reparation for slavery in the United States. Many African Americans claim that reparation is due from the European American descendants of slaveowners. Note two features associated with the existence of a *generational gap*, slavery having been formally abolished in 1865 in the US. First, today's descendants of slaveowners were unable to oppose their ancestors' clearly wrongful acts. Hence, they are not *causally* responsible for these abhorrent acts. Second, while persons are stuck within their period of existence, burdens and benefits can travel across generations.

What follows for claims of reparation for slavery? Such claims come in two forms. The *direct* one states that descendants should rectify as if they were wrongdoers. It assumes some sense of community-based continuity and collective moral responsibility across time. The *indirect* one claims that descendants should rectify to the extent that they *benefited* from past wrongdoing. It assumes the wrongfulness of sticking to wrongfully acquired benefits whenever current descendants of victims are worse off because of such past wrongs – and perhaps even when they are not. There is an extensive debate about the nature, justification, and plausibility of each of these *direct* and *indirect* rectificatory views.[3]

In a cross-generational world, the direct, "wrongdoer pays" claim is philosophically fragile beyond the overlap. It requires both causation and wrongdoing. However, current descendants and past wrongdoers never coexisted. Yet, as non-coexistence does not prevent the cross-generational transfer of burdens and benefits, the indirect, "beneficiary pays" route remains open and is seen by many authors as a plausible "second-best." "Beneficiary pays" requires beneficiaries from past wrongdoings to compensate the victims of such past wrongdoings *up to the level of* these benefits. The principle suffers a series of problems too, though. The main one is the following: why treat the slavery-generated benefits *separately* from benefits resulting from other sources, such as natural, political, or market luck experienced by our ancestors?

Why would rich descendants of slaveowners owe more
to slave descendants than luckier and possibly even richer
descendants of lucky industrials who would not have
been involved in slavery? The issue here is about how far
it is plausible to extend the scope of the idea of "unjust
enrichment" and the consequences we attach to it. Also,
why would poor descendants of slaveowners owe cash
to all descendants of slaves, including those who might
happen to have become richer than they are? Here, the
issue brings us back to how we want to articulate the
rectificatory and the distributive dimensions.

Current people carry deep wounds when their
community has suffered genocide, slavery, colonization,
or other appalling abuses in the past. The nature of our
responses (words, cash, structural reforms, etc.) and their
source (society as a whole, descendants of wrongdoers,
etc.) definitely matter to heal such wounds. When there
is more at stake in rectification than correcting mere
losses in *material* wealth, it may be tempting to tag and
isolate inherited benefits that are causally connected with
wrongful acts in the past, and to assign a symbolic role
to material transfers. Yet we face difficulties here that
are related to harm and causation, different from those
identified in chapter 1. Past slavery undoubtedly generated
harms and wrongs in the past. And the vast majority of
them were outside the scope of the non-identity problem.
Yet past harms do not automatically translate into current
wrongs if we find ourselves in a non-overlapping setting.
They may, but we need an account for this. We need an
explanation of why individuals with no (backward) causal
responsibility for past wrongful harms ought to be subject
to special blame. And this concern, while having to do
with the absence of coexistence with the victims, is not
necessarily related to the non-identity problem.

We need to identify meaningful and effective responses
to past wrongs as a matter of justice toward groups of
victims in the present and future. I am neither questioning
the wrongfulness of past slavery, nor expressing doubts

about the existence of current scars – despite the non-identity issues – nor challenging the idea that past slavery demands specific, unambiguous, and collective responses today, including through cash transfers. I am "merely" challenging the insistence on causal links with the past to identify who owes such responses today.

My core concern is whether descendants of wrongdoers have *special* obligations toward current victims of past wrongs, obligations that differ from those of society at large. Answering in the negative *does not* downplay the importance of what happened and of what is owed. For instance, when some terrorists claim to act in the name of a specific religion, many of us are reluctant to expect *special apologies* from the whole religious group at stake, even if we remain among contemporaries. The point is that the latter approach does not need to involve any denial of the suffering of past and current victims. It rather implies a view about *who* owes apologies.

So should we impose *special* duties on the descendants of wrongdoers in cases in which they were not adults when the acts took place? I think that we should lean toward a *negative* answer and that we should reframe our policies accordingly. Here is a sketch. The starting point involves a stylized fact and a moral principle. The *fact* is the existence of a generational gap – i.e. the "non-overlap" feature referred to above: descendants of wrongdoers never coexisted with the latter. This also circumscribes the scope of my claims below. The *moral principle* is that one should not be held morally responsible in a primary sense for acts that took place before one's birth – and even to some degree "before adulthood" – and for their consequences today. This echoes the common assumption in civil liability regimes that one should not be held liable for the consequences of others' acts unless one has some duty of control/supervision over them – as when parents are held responsible for the actions of their children who are minors. If we take "ought implies can" seriously, we cannot have any prenatal duties.[4]

The conjunction of this stylized fact and this moral principle calls for a reframing in two complementary directions. First, our duties to current and future victims of past wrongdoers should be phrased as much as possible as general duties, bearing on *all of us* – or to put it more precisely, on all current non-victims of these past acts. Second, as far as possible, we should go "distributive" rather than "rectificatory" when it comes to the material (as opposed to symbolic) dimensions of injustice. By "symbolic," I mean actions the *expressive* dimension of which is central, and I don't imply at all that they are unimportant – quite the contrary.

The first strategy consists in reframing special duties falling on specific groups as general duties falling on all of us but the current victims. To illustrate, I move from slavery to genocide. When Turkish authorities wrongfully deny facts about the 1916 Armenian genocide, we don't need to imply the existence of *special* duties associated with past wrong-doing. We can characterize this instead as the violation of a general duty of truthfulness that *any* community and any state authorities have today toward appalling past events of such significance. In addition, Turkish authorities may also be violating the duty falling on *any* country having *privileged access to information* about such appalling past events, regardless of whether its citizens in the past were causally involved. Moreover, beyond fact-finding, one should expect the firmest moral condemnation by current Turkish people and their authorities of such appalling past events, as well as their recognition as genocide. But this is again something that we might expect from members of *any* decent state. If a genocide took place, the authorities of countries other than Turkey should also recognize its existence, or at the very least not deny it. Finally, it seems to me that *empathy* toward current descendants suffering deeply from denial keeps making plenty of sense in our generational-gap-conscious setting.

A trickier issue is whether current Turkish people should *apologize*, given that hardly any of its current members had reached adult age in 1916. Apologies tend to presuppose guilt endorsement by ourselves, which goes beyond pointing to the guilt of others. Yet apologies are problematic for anyone denying that collective responsibility, understood in the strong sense of "guilt-endorsement," may extend to acts *anterior* to our very existence. Unfortunately, I cannot go more deeply into this here. I cannot discuss, for instance, alternative meanings of "apologies" or different accounts of collective responsibility. What matters here is that what I have just discussed gives us a rough idea about the – sometimes troubling – implications of part one of our generational-gap-conscious strategy. This is about specifying the nature of our duties to the present and the future, taking seriously the absence of overlap with the past.

What happens when moving *beyond symbolic measures* such as those we have just discussed, or *beyond structural measures* aimed at avoiding the repetition of past wrongs? The second part of our strategy is that when it comes to losses in *material wealth* resulting from wrongs *by past generations*, we should renounce the rectificatory strategy as far as possible when we find ourselves outside the overlap, and move more decidedly to a distributive one. The argument is twofold. First, if wrongs by past people are not wrongs by current people, then they ought to be treated as mere *past facts* as far as our non-symbolic, resource-focused duties are concerned. And if these wrongs are treated as past facts, there is no reason to *isolate* them from all the other morally (un)problematic past acts or events that caused current distributions of wealth. This does not mean that current distributions of wealth should be left as they are. It merely means that when correcting current *distributive* injustices, past wrongs should not be treated in isolation.

Second, some readers may fear that going distributive will *weaken* the importance of our duties of justice. This is an unjustified fear because, as far as external resources are concerned, rectification claims necessarily derive their strength from underlying distributive assumptions, as I stressed in chapter 1. If I owe you back a good that I took away from you, it is primarily because you were the legitimate owner of this good in the first place. Yet to establish whether you were the legitimate owner of it, one needs something like a theory of distributive justice. Hence, when it comes to external goods – as opposed to physical integrity or freedom of speech, for instance – the moral intensity of rectificatory claims is parasitic on the strength of background distributive claims. Shifting from a backward-looking, rectificatory approach to a forward-looking, distributive one is unlikely to weaken our claims of justice, even though the pool of duty-holders may be broader. The whole issue is of course to find out *what* distributive justice requires.

Does the anthropic nature of pre-1990 emissions matter?

What does this entail for the historical-emissions issue? I have shown that even in cases in which the wrongfulness of past acts is very clear, taking the generational gap seriously requires a reinterpretation of the nature of our current duties. Now, in the case of pre-1990 emissions, while the generational gap is narrower than for slavery in the US or for the Armenian genocide, the wrongfulness of the emissions is also more doubtful at least until the mid-twentieth century, given our past excusable climatic ignorance. Hence, if a principle such as "beneficiary pays" is philosophically fragile in clear-cut cases like past slavery or past genocide, it becomes even more so in the case of historical emissions, given excusable ignorance.[5] While fact-finding about past emissions and their current consequences may be part of our epistemic duties, a moral condemnation of these past emissions is harder to defend.

What follows? If we accept the significance of the generational gap for a large part of our pre-1990 emissions, the latter should in fact be treated as one among various determinants of our current climate. While recognizing the reality of such past human emissions matters for the causal analysis of current climate problems, I submit that we should not give a central role to past emissions when defining what we owe future generations and other communities today as a matter of climate justice. Leaving aside what historical emissions teach us about our ability to affect our climate, the fact that our current climate situation results to a significant part from emissions by past generations of humans does *not* change the nature of our climate duties from now on. This echoes the non-cleronomic turn sketched in chapter 2 to some extent, as well as the choice of climate baseline discussed below when presenting three views on distributive climate justice. To understand what is at stake, let me return to our two questions (Q1 and Q2) in reverse order.

Consider Q2. What do current generations owe the future in terms of climate justice? Do historical emissions matter in this respect? Imagine a hypothetical, climate-friendly world that differs from ours in three respects. It has a much deeper understanding of our climate. It developed a safe, cheap, and "nature-based" technology allowing for easy fine-tuning of the planet's average temperature. And its activities have always remained climate-neutral so far. Yet, despite these three differences, it finds itself in the same climate mess as ours, facing similarly alarming forecasts, due this time to a strictly natural phenomenon. Think about a phenomenon comparable to changes in the Earth's temperature associated with natural Milankovitch cycles, but with a much stronger magnitude. Here is our question: would the intergenerational climate duties of these climate friends differ from ours? In fact, I submit that they could be even *stronger* than ours, given the technology they have. If they can prevent their climate from getting worse for the next generations by relying on a technology that costs them hardly anything, they ought to do so as a matter of intergenerational climate justice. And the absence of (wrongful) human impact on the climate does not prevent such climate duties to the future from obtaining and from being significant.

Let me then move back to Q1. In our hypothetical climate-friendly world, there are also large differences among countries. Some territories are more climatically exposed and/or climatically vulnerable than others. Yet the climate mess that this climate-friendly world is undergoing is similar to ours. Does the absence of human causes of this climate mess prevent the existence of distributive obligations to countries that are climatically more exposed or vulnerable? I don't think so. A proper understanding of climate justice, coupled with an appropriate conception of global justice, namely justice across countries, should defend such duties. I submit, indeed, that these obligations are likely to be even stronger than those grounded in a principle such as "beneficiary pays" – on top of being philosophically more robust. And this is true for the hypothetical world I imagined, but also for our own world.

Hence, my answer to both Q1 and Q2 is negative. It takes the implications of non-overlap seriously. Historical emissions remain key to understanding our climate and the role and responsibility of humankind. They also clearly render our duties even more daunting, as for any other cause worsening our present and future climate. However, they are not a source of *special* obligations falling on specific groups because of their special links with those who emitted more in the past. Claiming that affluent countries have stronger climate duties than less affluent ones does not need to invoke the fact that the former's ancestors emitted more than the latter's. Claiming that current generations have stronger duties than future ones does not need to invoke the fact that the former are closer relatives of the authors of historical emissions.[6] Nor should we draw the implication that there is no room left for climate rectificatory duties. They remain crucial *among contemporaries*, whenever we violate our climate duties.

Finally, answering "no" to Q1 and Q2 about special climate duties associated with historical emissions does *not* mean that our climate duties become undifferentiated or insignificant, as we are now going to show. It is just their justification that changes.

Distributive climate justice: three views

All this is plausible if we take seriously the notion of *distributive* climate justice. This also implies being lucid about *what* distributive climate justice requires. Let me contrast three understandings of the latter, all three potentially applying domestically, globally, and cross-generationally. These versions of *distributive climate justice* (DCJ) can be phrased as follows:

We ought to prevent or compensate unjust disadvantages resulting from ...

... *human-induced* climate circumstances (DCJ1)
... human-induced *or natural* climate circumstances (DCJ2)
... human-induced or natural circumstances, in allocating *climate-related rights* (DCJ3)

Let me begin with DCJ1. At first sight, one may think that issues of climate justice only arise because humans started having a significant influence on the natural climate. Assuming that a natural climate does not raise issues of justice is perhaps due to reducing climate justice to its rectificatory version. Yet, on reflection, natural disasters such as hurricanes or floods clearly raise issues of distributive justice too, even in the absence of any human-induced global warming.[7] This does not mean that there should be no room for rectificatory climate justice at all when human action is at stake, especially among contemporaries. It merely means that we need more than DCJ1 as a plausible account of distributive climate justice. We need a version that does not leave differences in *natural* climate circumstances unaddressed.

Shifting to DCJ2 means that naturally adverse climate circumstances also matter for justice. This is what allowed us to develop the account presented above and to treat human-induced global warming inherited from the past as if it were natural *without* entailing the absence of distributive duties. For *global* climate justice, this means that we should go beyond addressing the consequences of human-induced climate change. We should extend climate justice to whether a country has an overall more favorable natural climate than another, irrespective of whether sea rise, drought, flooding, etc. can be traced back to human activities. For *intergenerational* climate justice, this means that each generation should envisage its climate duties to the next generation independently of whether the expected differences between the climate we experience and the climate that the next generation(s) will experience result from past human activity or rather from past, present, or forecast natural causes.

Note here that some may hold the view that there is a certain degree of choice in our vulnerability to climate change. Relocating urbanization to more climate-resilient locations, for instance to places more sheltered from sea rise, could sometimes be considered a duty of potentially affected countries. I am not discussing the plausibility of such claims here. I merely want to insist on the fact that as far as *generations* are concerned, there is no way in which we may relocate temporally to other (future or past) periods that would be forecast to be milder. Generations are time-locked. They are stuck in their period of existence and cannot even zap time segments of their lives that they expect to be climatically more extreme.[8]

DCJ1 and DCJ2 focus on climate circumstances, be they human-induced or not. Yet our condition as individuals, communities, or generations is also affected by numerous non-climatic determinants. There is one way in which this is acknowledged in the climate debate. The degree to which a community suffers from adverse climate change is not merely a function of its territory's exposure to climate conditions. It also depends on the ability of this community to react and adapt to climate events, which requires knowledge, technology, money, etc. Hence, it interacts with broader inequalities. A climate regime concerned about both mitigation and adaptation should take this into account.

DCJ3 goes one step further, though. It claims that climate justice should not merely *neutralize* the effects of climate change on general inequalities or on the least well-off, including those being left below sufficiency as a result of climate change. Neutralization means that we should make sure that climate change and the policies it requires do not *worsen* existing inequalities or disadvantages. DCJ3 assigns to climate justice a more *proactive* role. It claims that we should seize the existence of a global climate regime as an opportunity to contribute to meeting the demands of sufficiency and to further reduce unjust inequalities or disadvantages, even if they are *not* caused by climate circumstances. It uses the "climate rights" encapsulated in a climate regime (emission rights, rights to technology transfer, etc.) as a "commodity" to implement the domestic, global, and intergenerational justice agenda in general. This approach is especially plausible in a context such as the global one in which no general redistributive mechanism such as tax-and-transfer is in place.

It is beyond the scope of this chapter to engage in a *defense* of DCJ3.[9] Suffice it to mention three elements at this stage. First, blocking the move from the "isolationist" DCJ1 and DCJ2 to an approach in terms of DCJ3 is philosophically far from simple.[10] Hence, readers should not simply assume that DCJ3 is more "extreme" or "less natural" than the other two. And readers should keep in mind that this kind of issue arises whenever we want to apply a general theory of justice to a good-specific regime, be it about climate, mobility, housing, education, etc. It raises the general question of how to divide (re)distributive labor between policies.

Second, the argument I developed about the moral role of pre-1990 emissions is more at home with DCJ2 than with DCJ1, even though some interpretations of the latter might endorse it too. But the claim about its limited moral importance certainly does not *require* us to endorse DCJ3, even if the latter is compatible with it.

Third, there is a complex relationship between going for DCJ3 and the issue of trading some climate degradation against other benefits such as more efficient technologies. On the one hand, accepting *some* substitution of climate quality with other benefits will render it harder to oppose DCJ3, since that version refuses to insulate a climate regime from broader concerns about justice. By "broader," I am referring to concerns that go beyond *avoiding the worsening* of existing inequalities and disadvantages. On the other hand, rejecting any substitution of climate quality for other benefits *does not* prevent us from endorsing DCJ3. One can perfectly well claim that one should uncompromisingly stick to a natural climate (or to a globally optimal climate even if it differs from our natural climate) and at the same time incorporate non-climate redistributive concerns in allocating the rights and duties required by one's climate target. Our global emissions target and the way in which we distribute the effort to reach it are to some degree autonomous. This shows how complex these matters are.

Emissions in the past, duties to the future

I will return to the substitution issue below. Meanwhile, what to conclude on historical emissions? Non-overlap and excusable ignorance converge to support a case for a forward-looking approach that severs our duties to the future from strings of moral blame from the past. One ought to ask what distributive climate justice *from now on* requires, regardless of undeniable pre-1990 human causes of our current and future climate mess. The content of such "duties from now on" depends on several bifurcations. First, the precise contours of our distributive view depend on the type of principle of justice we endorse, as discussed in chapter 2. Second, our climate duties depend on metrics-related issues. How to identify whether something is a disadvantage under DCJ? And may climate degradation be traded against energy efficiency improvements, for instance? This brings us back to the issues discussed in chapter 3. Third, the content of our duties from now on also depends on the role assigned to a climate regime in promoting justice, which we approached through contrasting three views. Our forward-looking approach is more at home with DCJ2 than with DCJ1, while also clearly compatible with DCJ3.

In the end, do pre-1990 emissions raise a truly intergenerational issue? What is at stake is the significance of acts by past generations for the definition of current generations' duties. Yet one could argue that this "merely" raises issues of justice *within* generations, between the descendants of past harm-doers and current victims. In fact, our treatment of Q1 and Q2 shows that issues of *intergenerational* justice clearly arise too. For it is about what current members of some communities owe current *and future* members of other communities. More importantly, it is also about what we owe the future as a generation as a whole.

A strictly rectificatory approach to past emissions could actually limit the climate duties of current generations to the future to the effects of our *own* emissions. Our climate duties to the future would then be limited to avoiding uncompensated *further* harms compared with a baseline scenario under which *current* generations would not have emitted anything. This would mean denying the current generations any duty of justice to the future with respect to the long-lasting effects of pre-1990 emissions on future people. The future impacts of "runaway trains" launched in the past would not be our problem, even if such impacts are real if we consider the most long-lived greenhouse gases.

In contrast, our distributive account acknowledges the effects of past emissions on future climate. If future generations will predictably experience a worse climate than ours, we would have climate duties to them *even if* climate worsening were *not* mainly due to our own emissions. Hence, historical emissions raise plain issues of duties *to the future*. Arguably, it is the move to explicitly forward-looking and distributive accounts that renders this salient. The case of runaway trains launched in the past also confirms the need to move away from a strictly inheritance-focused perspective, as stressed in chapter 2. For if such trains were inherited, a no-decline approach might, under some of its interpretations, not expect us to try and stop them or to compensate the future. This is so because their predicted future harms were already "set," in a sense, when we came to existence. This would clearly be counterintuitive, for example if the runaway train is expected to destroy more lives in the future than in the present.

Can climate degradation be fair to the future?

I have explored the significance of historical emissions for our duties to the future. Let me move to our second focal point: the idea of not going beyond a long-term surface mean global temperature increase of 2°C compared with preindustrial times. This requires a radical adjustment of our emission trajectories. Unsurprisingly, given its significance, whether the target is set right is a debated matter.[11] Moreover, whether a global and long-term temperature target is more apt to trigger the local and short-term policy responses needed than more specific targets for greenhouse gas concentration is debatable.[12] Here, I want to explore how a theory of intergenerational justice should approach such a *global temperature target*. It is key for the climate that current and future generations will experience. It is equally key for the mitigation and adaptation effort expected from current and future generations.

We can approach a global temperature increase from a transition (climate change) and/or from an end-state (climate degradation) perspective. Both are intergenerationally relevant. From a transition perspective, an issue of intergenerational justice potentially arises regardless of whether the business-as-usual or the targeted-average emission level *is worse or not* than preindustrial levels. The focus is on the climate *change* dimension, and on the distribution of fair transition costs across transition generations, especially when *fast* changes require fast reactions. Hence, I understand "transition" in a narrower sense than in e.g. "ecological transition." In contrast, from an end-state perspective, our concern for global warming does not reduce to transition concerns. A warmer global climate is a *worse* climate, overall. Going above a 2°C increase has been described as "dangerous."[13] Here, I will focus on the end-state dimension, even if the size and distribution of transition costs matter too and are central to transition studies.

Also, setting a 2°C (or even a 1.5°C) target neither *exclusively* flows from forecasts from the natural *sciences*, nor implies that a *natural* climate is always a better climate. There is no objection from the natural sciences to aiming at a 1°C rather than at a 2°C target. The target involves a political and *normative* choice, albeit informed by natural and social sciences. In fact, there is an interesting history behind the 2°C figure.[14] It makes sense to scrutinize it from the perspective of a theory of intergenerational justice, as it is one of the core components of the climate regime. Similarly, given our limited understanding of natural phenomena and the magnitude of the forces at play, it is wise to think twice before departing from *natural* global temperatures. Yet the very fact of allowing for a 2°C *increase* necessarily implies as such that we do not assume that natural systems should be left untouched, or that a generation should reset the climate to its preindustrial state at any cost. More generally, if we were moving fast to a *natural* global warming of the same speed and magnitude as ours, we would probably not be standing idly by for the mere reason that it is natural.

It is crucial to understand the place of a long-term climate target in light of a principle of justice and in light of an explicit metrics. Arguably, even in the best compliance scenario, we are globally aiming at a target such that the global climate for the next generations will be worse, less habitable, than ours. This is so even if we remain below the 2°C rise, which is looking increasingly unlikely as we are already above 1°C warming. To justify leaving to the next generation a climate system that is significantly *worse* than ours, we need to imagine provisos potentially allowing for fairness-based defenses. Here are four possible options likely to pop up in the public debate and that are worth envisaging:

A 2°C climate degradation can be intergenerationally fair if ...

Non-responsibility proviso
... it results from inertia, lock-in, and runaway effects triggered by natural phenomena or by past emissions, for which current people are not causally responsible.

Sufficiency proviso
... it does not prevent future generations from covering their basic needs.

Efficiency proviso
... avoiding such degradation would be (massively) inefficient, considering the well-being of both current and future generations.

Substitutability proviso
… it is compensated by improvements in other respects, regardless of whether they contribute to our climate adaptation abilities or improve our lives in other ways.

Let me go through each of these provisos. I argued above at length why rejecting our responsibility for past events *does not* necessarily commit us to the non-responsibility proviso. As soon as we remember that distributive duties do not presuppose a prior harm as a trigger, DCJ2 offers a clear alternative allowing us to drop the non-responsibility proviso. The fact that climate degradations are inherited from the past, be they human-induced or not, does not necessarily leave them outside the scope of our climate duties. This entails that non-responsibility turns out not to be a promising candidate for justifying a 2°C degradation.

What about the sufficiency proviso? While it might seem more promising, on both the sufficientarian justice and the sufficientarian sustainability fronts, it leaves two important questions open. One is whether the extent of climate degradation allowed for by the 2°C target is effectively compatible with *meeting the demands* of sufficiency, especially if we consider the possibility of future non-compliance by coming generations. There are not many grounds for optimism on this front. The other is that sufficiency may offer a very incomplete account of the demands of distributive justice, for instance for someone endorsing prioritarianism or leximin egalitarianism above the threshold. For such a more complex view – more in line with what many domestic systems are aiming at – meeting the demands of the sufficiency proviso is not enough.

Those unsatisfied with merely meeting the sufficiency proviso are left with two further provisos, one touching upon the *principle* of justice that we endorse, and the other having to do with the *metrics* of our conception of justice. I will be brief on efficiency because we will come back to it in the next section, but also because, while there is plausibility in expecting early efforts in the name of efficiency, as we shall see, it is far less straightforward to expect that there may be much efficiency to gain from letting our climate degrade for generations to come. So the efficiency proviso is unlikely to be able to justify a 2°C degradation, given the number of generations ahead that will suffer these effects. Admittedly, there is more room for efficiency concerns in a theory of justice that is prioritarian or leximin egalitarian than in one that is more plainly egalitarian, and that cares about inequalities as such as opposed to the maximal improvement of the least well-off. But even for the theories that allow more leeway to efficiency, putting the burden later is likely to be less efficient than putting it earlier.

If we leave aside political feasibility grounds for allowing for a 2°C degradation, the key proviso thus seems to be the *substitutability* one. Unfortunately, as indicated in the previous chapter, substitutability is a tricky issue, especially if approached from a liberal perspective that considers that our social arrangements should rest as little as possible on the conception of the good that one may have about the intrinsic value of a great landscape, or about the aesthetic value of biodiversity.[15] A liberal approach may frame the issue in that way. And we may conclude that it has nothing very profound to say about substitutability. This does not mean, of course, that nothing worthwhile can be said about aesthetic or intrinsic value. It simply means that these thoughts should not be factored into a *political* theory of intergenerational justice. In addition, it is true that the contours of the just/ good distinction are far from set, for instance when we ask whether the debate on the dignity of wild animals is a matter of justice or belongs to debates between conceptions of the good. Note finally that once we accept that some climate degradation can be traded against improvements in other respects, we still haven't said anything about whether such compensation is actually taking place. What we can conclude at this stage is that justifying a 2°C degradation requires the acceptance of substitutability.

While it is necessary for such justification, it is not clear whether the demands for actual substitution will actually be met. If not, even meeting the 2°C target, which seems very unlikely at this stage, would be insufficient to meet this demand of intergenerational justice.

Can early efforts be fair to the present?

I have just touched upon the efficiency dimension. By efficiency, I am not referring to Pareto efficiency but rather to cost-effectiveness, broadly construed, i.e. the idea of reaching a given goal at the lowest possible cost. This can allow for a larger amount of total well-being in society, including cross-generationally, irrespective of the distribution of this well-being. As mentioned in the previous chapter, most theories of justice are sensitive to efficiency, each in its own way. Utilitarianism gives efficiency the most central role. Yet leximin egalitarians, for instance, value efficiency gains to the extent that these benefit the least well-off. It is unclear how much efficiency played a significant role in setting the 2°C target. Considering the number of generations ahead that might have benefited, a lower global target might arguably have been more efficient.

Besides being used to define a global temperature target, efficiency can also play a role in setting the trajectory of reductions aimed at meeting the demands of the global target. *Early effort* seems especially efficient.[16] One reason is that the sooner we engage in the sprawling learning process required to reach a carbon-neutral society, the faster we are likely to reach it. Another reason is that the sooner we react, the less the further accumulation of greenhouse gases, hence the less the need for even more radical mitigation or further adaptation.

Let me assume that early effort is indeed cross-generationally efficient and that it would also have been cross-generationally efficient to set the climate target below 2°C. This raises a challenge for *distributive* theories of justice. For the costs and benefits associated with a policy may not be simultaneous. As we have said, there are front-loaded goods (benefits first, costs after) and back-loaded ones (costs first, benefits after). One may worry about the undersupply of back-loaded goods and the oversupply of front-loaded goods.[17] Nuclear energy, with use today and swimming pools of highly radioactive waste to manage for thousands of future years, is a front-loaded good. Blue-sky research, with decades of research leading to benefits for centuries, is a back-loaded good.

The problem is not that a given generation will not reap the full benefits of its own efforts. This may be a concern for direct-reciprocity advocates, but not necessarily for distributive views. The problem is rather that we may be asking the poorest generations to put in the most effort, the benefits of which will moreover fall primarily on future and richer generations. We ask early generations to tighten their belt for the sake of later generations that are expected to be wealthier if we follow the policy at hand. We are back to the core concern driving the "narrow path" view in chapter 2.

How to address this? There are at least three ways, which could be labeled "substitution," "priority relaxation," and "unavoidable decline." I begin with the first one. One could argue for compensating the future benefits associated with early climate action with future burdens that would be counterparts of current benefits. We could be investing massively in decarbonation today, with very significant benefits for the future, while enjoying nuclear energy today, leaving the burden of nuclear waste management to the future. This is substitution *in kind*.

Substitution is harder to achieve *in cash* if we consider *closed* economies. As stressed in chapter 2, funding a policy through a long-term debt does not necessarily shift costs to the future, if generations are taken as wholes, at the global level. What indebtedness does is to expect one segment of a generation (current lenders) to tighten its belt for another segment of the same generation (current borrowers), under the assumption that one segment of the next generation (the descendants of current lenders) will get the money "back" from another segment of the next generation (the descendants of current borrowers). Hence, running a debt in cash is only an option if the money is not lent by one's own citizens, in which case we would simply be shifting money from one part of society to another part of society without any generational transfers. As a planetary economy, running a financial debt does *not* operate any transfer *between* generations, even though it operates transfers *within* generations *across* time.[18]

So, if we engage in the production of *back-loaded climate initiatives*, future people will not be able to share the climate-related benefits with us once we have passed away. Also, we are unable to anticipatively grab such future climate-related benefits and bring them back to the present, as they don't exist yet. Moreover, while such climate initiatives can either be seen as ways of *benefiting* the future or as ways of *not burdening* the future *further*, this does not make a major difference for a distributive view that cares about overall packages of opportunities. Then, while running a *cash* debt is not a very promising avenue for the reasons just alluded to, "compensation" *in kind* is certainly an option, either through depriving the future of other benefits (e.g. exploit today some really useful non-renewable resources in a climate-neutral way) or through imposing on the future other burdens (e.g. leave them nuclear waste that can be managed in a climate-neutral way if nuclear energy makes a lot of sense today). This may actually be required by the "narrow path" view. The crucial thing will be to avoid any form of wasteful substitution in kind.

A second way to justify early action consists in relaxing the priority to the least well-off. Benefits of early effort may be so massive, considering how many generations will benefit in the future, that even if this entails worsening the condition of the least well-off across generations

– assuming here that they will be members of the early-effort generation – the overall gains are such that this should trump the distributive concern. This position is not at all absurd even if it departs from the "narrow path" spirit. The problem is, of course, that once we consider how many issues may involve massive benefits to the future, even a slight departure from a priority to the least well-off could significantly empty the distributive logic of its practical substance, unless we limit ourselves to a finite horizon of one or two centuries. For it is reasonable to assume that the current generation's population is otherwise only a tiny segment of the larger population including us and the future.

While early climate efforts seem to be the way to go, they are not straightforward to justify if we assume that earlier generations tend to be the least well-off and if we advocate a strong priority to the least well-off. The third way out challenges the former rather than the latter of these two assumptions. It postulates that the least well-off are likely to be in the future rather than the present. This does not necessarily require seeing early effort and the time location of the least well-off as independent from one another. Yet it assumes at least that early climate-related efforts, even if fully implemented, would remain unable to address the climate challenge enough for technology improvements in other respects to keep us within an overall non-decline. If we find ourselves in such an unavoidable decline scenario, then early effort would of course be easy to justify, not only on efficiency grounds, but also out of concern for the least well-off, intergenerationally.

Can a positive social discount rate be fair to the future?

There is one last intergenerational issue to discuss here. When policy makers weigh burdens and benefits distributed across time and associated with alternative long-term policies, they apply a *social discount factor*.[19] The practice has long raised ethical concerns. Back in 1928, British philosopher and mathematician Franck Ramsey expressed this concern in a seminal paper, when in presenting his model he said that the practice is "ethically indefensible and arises merely from the weakness of the imagination," while suggesting the need for nuance.[20] In climate policy, the level at which we set the social discounting rate is of major practical significance. Consider, for instance, John Broome's account of the Nicholas Stern vs. William Nordhaus debate a few years back:

> The discount rate measures how fast the value of goods diminishes with time … . Nordhaus discounts at roughly 6 percent a year; Stern discounts at 1.4 percent. The effect is that Stern gives a present value of $247 billion for having, say, a trillion dollars' worth of goods a century from now. Nordhaus values having those same goods in 2108 at just $2.5 billion today. Thus Stern attaches nearly 100 times as much value as Nordhaus to having any given level of costs and benefits 100 years from now.[21]

In short, here is a component of climate policy that involves an intergenerational dimension, raises ethical concerns, and carries very significant practical implications. This surely requires a closer look, with the aim of understanding the practice, assessing it, and bridging it with the considerations of justice developed earlier. To understand and assess "social discounting" one can frame it as involving two core components, i.e. an object (*"what* is being discounted?") and a reason (*"why* are we discounting it?"). Let us compare the following four types of discounting, sometimes combined in actual calculations:

D1: discounting future *consumption* for *diminishing marginal well-being.*
D2: discounting future *well-being* for *diminishing marginal moral importance of well-being.*

D3: discounting future *well-being* for *uncertainty about future existence of persons*.
D4: discounting future *well-being* for *time distance*.

Let me present the core intuitions driving each of these and assess whether they violate *impartiality* across time, impartiality being key to most – if not all – theories of justice. Consider D1: one unit of *consumption* today is worth *more* for a social planner than one future unit of consumption. This rests on *four* assumptions. First, it assumes that future people *will be* wealthier than we are. Second, it implies that the wealthier one is, the less an extra unit of consumption can bring extra well-being. An apple generates more additional well-being if allocated to the hungry than to the well fed. Third, it requires that our *metrics* of justice incorporates some degree of welfarism, rendering it sensitive to "diminishing marginal well-being" effects. Fourth, it presupposes that our *principle* of justice grants some weight to aggregative concerns, rendering it sensitive to the view that consumption should be located whenever it generates *the most* happiness.

What about D2? Under D1, future consumption is being discounted because of its lesser contribution to well-being. Under D2, we discount future units of well-being rather than of consumption. This does not need to imply that future persons matter less than us. Nor does it even entail that future well-being necessarily matters less than well-being today. Rather, it rests on two assumptions. First, it endorses the *moral* claim that the happier you are, the less society should care about increasing your happiness further. One should be concerned as a priority about improving the well-being of those with a lesser level of well-being. This can be referred to as the *value judgment* that *well-being* has a diminishing marginal *moral* importance, independently of whether it holds true that *consumption* generates diminishing marginal benefits for well-being as a matter of *fact*. Second, D2 rests on a factual assumption, i.e. the prediction that average levels of well-being will increase over time.

Whether D1 and D2 make sense partly depends on whether future people will turn out to be, respectively, richer or happier than us, which depends on ... our policies. Yet the *normative* assumptions at work in D1 and D2 do not necessarily violate impartiality between us and the future. Admittedly, there might be different normative readings of what impartiality requires, for instance depending on which mix of distributive and aggregative concerns best characterizes its demands. However, they do not need to violate impartiality.

For D3 and D4, both *distance* between us and them (D4) and *uncertainty* about the very existence of future people (D3) matter. These dimensions are less contingent than the truth value of assumptions about future people's levels of wealth (D1) or happiness (D2). In both the D3 and D4 cases, the passage of time and its associated features are meant to affect our obligations toward the future. Does adjusting our duties to the future on such a basis entail that future people matter less, morally speaking, hence violating impartiality?

Let me begin with D3. We could think that we have stronger duties to people who exist *for sure* than to people who merely *may* exist. And we could add that the more distant in the future possible people are, the higher the risk that they might never come into existence. The passage of time increases the probability of existential threats to humankind. This form of discounting does not need to endorse the view that future people matter less than we do. What it does is rather to orient our duties to closer humans *because* their very existence is less uncertain. D3 can claim to treat members of other generations as equals *proportionally to* the degree to which their very existence – i.e. the continuation of humankind – is certain or not.

D4 also cares about time distance, while leaving things open about reasons for which it may matter morally. In a sense, D3 can be seen as a subtype of D4. Whether

D4 is compatible with respecting future people as equals depends *on the reasons* associated with distance and invoked to justify discounting. Simply claiming that future people matter less for some "far from the eyes, far from the heart" reason will not do for anyone concerned with impartiality.

By way of illustration, comparing the temporal with the spatial realm, we could explore one possible ground for D4 by trying an analogy with strategies adopted by specific types of nationalists. Is the view that we have stronger duties toward our co-nationals compatible with some form of impartiality across nations? It could be driven by a sense of division of *political* labor. One could be a *moral* cosmopolitan while endorsing *political* nationalism along subsidiarity (or "division of labor") lines. We would be assuming that certain tasks are better achieved at one level than at another. Under this view, people from other countries matter *morally* as much as our co-citizens. However, our *political* duties toward them – namely those that should be enforceable through taxation, for instance – are much more limited than those toward our co-nationals – or so the view would say. If we make sure that each nation has equal means of taking care of its citizens, such a view might not be completely implausible. Yet such a "subsidiarity nationalism" becomes implausible in a world of massive global inequalities.

Consider an analogous "subsidiarity generationalism" as an attempt at supporting D4 in an impartiality-preserving way. We could consider subsidiarity across generational *overlaps*. While people with whom we don't overlap would not morally matter less than overlappers, our ability to harm or benefit the latter is stronger, because of what physical coexistence allows for. This could justify differentiated political duties, depending on whether we interact with people with whom we overlap or not. Overlaps differ from borders or distance. Yet they are not unrelated. Generations overlapping during a given period of time share a temporal "territory" to some extent. In contrast, there is an uncrossable border between non-overlapping generations, which we referred to earlier as the generational gap. Also, since people's existence is short, the more time passes, the more it separates us, which points to a connection between distance and non-overlap. Yet one challenge to subsidiarity nationalism is typically how it handles policies with a cross-national dimension, such as pollution in international watercourses or trade restrictions. And the kinds of policies that we worry about from an intergenerational perspective *all* have this cross-periodic dimension that renders the subsidiarity response moot. As a result, it is likely that D4 – with the exception of D3 if seen as an instance of it – will be hard to render compatible with impartiality across periods.

Besides the compatibility of different types of discounting with the idea of impartiality, it is also worth reconnecting the issue of discounting with the substantive views explored in chapters 2 and 3. Consider the "narrow path" view. It will question two assumptions of D1. First, insofar as we endorse the *normative* standpoint of a prohibition on generational savings, we will be in trouble with the *factual* assumption according to which future people will be wealthier than we are. I am not claiming here that a normative claim can question the veracity of a prediction, but rather that the latter will be in violation of what the normative view commends. To put it differently, the problem is that discounting cannot be applied to determine the size of the *full* basket of what we transfer to future generations. For it is precisely the size of this basket that will determine whether future people will be wealthier than us. It is, then, problematic to define the levels of wealth of the various generations *independently* of the social discount rate, since the former will depend on the latter if that is applied to our intergenerational transfers as a whole. We cannot presuppose accumulation *before* setting the level of the discount rate while at the same time risking setting the rate at such a level that it will prevent accumulation.

Second, locating goods or tasks in time where they would generate the largest increases in well-being is driven by an aggregative concern that partly departs from the core of the "narrow path" view. The latter is primarily driven by a concern for maximizing the situation of the least well-off – as opposed to the *total* amount of well-being across generations. And this takes place in a context in which welfare gains cannot easily be redistributed across time, as discussed earlier.

I have not aimed here to present a conclusive argument about social discounting. The point has rather been to stress that this practice may take significantly different forms. We need to understand what is being discounted and for what reasons. And we then need to bridge it with our general theory of intergenerational justice.

Conclusion

Climate injustice is an issue of major concern. While the intergenerational dimension is central to only part of the questions that climate policy raises, they are both philosophically and practically significant. I have looked, essentially, into four questions: historical emissions, climate degradation, early effort, and the social discount rate.[22]

On historical emissions, I stressed how much difference adopting a distributive rather than a rectificatory approach can make, especially for those taking the generational gap seriously. I emphasized that distributive climate justice can be understood in three very different ways. This raises the essential question of what role to assign to a domain-specific regime within a more general objective of justice. In addition, I also showed that historical emissions are relevant to intergenerational justice per se (Q2) and not only to justice between communities across time (Q1).

On the 2°C target and on early effort, I showed how important the issue of substitution is, which touches upon the metrics dimension explored in chapter 3. I also discussed the intersection with efficiency concerns in both cases, and how efficiency can be factored into our general distributive approach. In the end, while neither 2°C nor early effort are straightforward to justify, they essentially raise the question of how to weigh potentially huge efficiency gains for a very large population of future people against concern for a much smaller and arguably less well-off population found in present generations. This was already central in the "narrow path" discussion in chapter 2.

Finally, I provided some elements with which to approach the technical debate on the social discount rate. Here, what is key is to understand exactly what is being discounted and which reasons support such discounting. The practice plays an essential role in climate policy. And one should keep an eye on the extent to which a discounting practice is compatible both with impartiality across generations in general, and with distributive demands.

5

Can policies be *legitimate* toward the future?

This book is about intergenerational *justice*, and more specifically about distributive justice between birth cohorts. It is about its possibility, its meaning, and its specificities. Until now, I have not said much about *institutional design*. It can be approached from the angle of distributive justice and from the perspective of democratic *legitimacy*. I will not engage here with the details of intergenerational institutional design.[1] What I want to do instead is to provide a few basic tools for how the intergenerational dimension of institutional design should be approached through the prism of normative political philosophy. For that purpose, I will pay special attention to the distinction between justice and legitimacy, as well as to the distinction (and articulation) between overlapping and non-overlapping generations contexts.

Before I proceed, note how non-identity, non-existence, and *non-coexistence* have accompanied us throughout the various chapters of this book. In chapter 1, the non-identity problem was central. Yet "Who will exist in the future?" differs from "Will someone exist in the future?" In chapter 4, our discussion of the social discount rate stressed that uncertainties about the very existence of humans in the future may matter for justice. In chapter 2, I also discussed whether justice requires that there *ought* to be people after us. "*Will* someone exist in the future?"

differs from "*Should* someone exist in the future?" Besides non-identity and non-existence, what follows from the fact that future people don't *coexist* with us? The overlap turned out to be crucial for the second strategy addressing the non-identity problem. Our non-coexistence with future people is also challenging for a preferentialist metrics, and our non-coexistence with past people matters to our treatment of historical emissions. Here I will explore what the absence of coexistence entails for democratic legitimacy.[2]

Distributive justice and democratic legitimacy

I begin with a few words about the distinction between distributive justice and democratic legitimacy. I take them to be at least partly independent. Distinguishing justice from legitimacy is not self-evident. Both aim at defining requirements that should be met to entitle a state to restrict the freedom of its citizens. Justice focuses more on the quality of *outcomes* of a certain type while legitimacy is rather concerned about features of decision-making *processes*. Political scientists often use the labels "output vs. input legitimacy" to refer, respectively, to outcome fairness and to process legitimacy. In contrast, public discourse often merges things, for instance when using "democratization" to refer to both decision-making processes and equal access to opportunities – as in "democratizing access to higher education."

There is a rich debate about what democracy and justice are, about whether they overlap, whether one is a subset of the other, or whether the value of one reduces to its instrumental value for the other.[3] To give the reader a sense of the complexity at stake, here are a few of the ways in which we may understand their relationship. First, "democratic egalitarians" define what we owe each other as a matter of justice, through reference to what people ought to enjoy to be able to properly interact as active citizens in a democracy.[4] Here, justice is to some degree meant to *serve* democracy. Second, operationalizing a preferentialist metrics of justice may rely on real proxies for hypothetical mechanisms. One way to achieve this consists in relying on the democratic forum to identify what should be seen as a disadvantage for the purposes of e.g. health care or housing policy. Here, we depend on a democratic procedure *to find out about* the demands of justice, to reveal preferences and their intensity.

Third, some views about democracy simply consider themselves as concerned with the fair distribution of a specific good, namely political power. Here, democracy becomes *one of the domains* of justice. Fourth, a *liberal egalitarian* theory of justice endorses the priority of basic freedoms over the goal of equalizing socio-economic opportunities. Hence, it values freedom of expression, for example. Here, justice and democracy *share* a core component. Fifth, there is a debate about who should be recognized as a member of the demos entitled to vote and mandate political decisions on a given territory or on a given issue. Yet excluding some people from a democratic decision-making process does not necessarily free us from duties of justice toward them. For instance, the legitimacy of locating a nuclear power plant does not necessarily require that residents from other potentially affected territories be granted a vote.[5] Yet this does not free us from duties of justice toward them. Here, the domain of justice *extends beyond* that of legitimacy.

These are five of the ways of conceptualizing the relationship between (distributive) justice and (democratic) legitimacy. Besides, there is also a rich body of empirical research on the extent to which socio-economic inequalities threaten democratic decision-making, for instance through campaign finance, and, conversely, on whether the choice of a given decision process tends to better promote distributive justice. These are just a few angles on the matter. I cannot provide a full account of how to

articulate justice and legitimacy conceptually, axiologically, normatively, or empirically. I will limit myself here
to the following assumptions.

I take legitimacy to mean "input legitimacy" and more
specifically "democratic legitimacy." I will also operate
with not-too-rich definitions of justice and democracy.
This allows us to distinguish them from one another. This
distinction matters because it forces us to render explicit
the nature of their relationships, to explore possible
tensions between them, and to find out about the degree
to which it is practically plausible to expect one without
the other. Going for a not-too-rich account of each does
not mean that democracy ought to be reduced to majority
rule, though. Other components, such as the inclusiveness
of a democracy's electoral franchise, the range of its
political liberties, the rule of law, the constitutionalization
of a significant set of its rights, a more or less watertight
separation of powers, a proper balance between the forum
(deliberation) and the market, etc. are key elements as
well, even for the "compact" notion of democracy that
I will rely upon here. I will certainly assume here that
democracies may reach decisions that are distributively
unfair (and unfortunately often do so). And I will assume
that they do this for reasons that cannot fully be traced
to violations of process legitimacy. Conversely, I will also
assume that dictatorships can sometimes come up with
policies that are distributively fair.

A voiceless and toothless future

What core challenges do future people raise for institutional
design if the latter is concerned about legitimacy? I begin
with a simplified democratic setting with non-overlapping
generations. I assume first – heroically – that citizens vote
impartially *and* that we merely want to *aggregate* their
respective political preferences through a fair procedure.
Aggregation faces serious problems. The specific difficulty

here is that, even if we can anticipate some of their core needs, we do not know the content and intensity of future people's preferences. Will future people value material heritage more than immaterial, cultural heritage more than natural, etc.? In addition, how to handle possibly mutually incompatible preferences of successive future generations? Admittedly, we could try and guess their preferences through general knowledge about human nature, evidence-based prediction, and anticipatory imagination. We may also want to influence the content of their values through exemplarity and education, as seen in chapter 3. Yet people to be born a century ahead of us are *voiceless* toward us, which reduces our ability to *understand* what they may want, even if their preferences partly result from our own actions and even if they are mutually compatible.

Consider, then, a slightly different world. Here, citizens remain exclusively geared toward the common good. What changes is one of the core functions assigned to a democracy. Rather than being about aggregating preexisting preferences, democracy is about setting up *deliberation* fora, potentially transforming some of our respective values. In contrast with bargaining, deliberation involves articulating and sharing *reasons* supporting our views, potentially helping each other filter them through such an exchange.[6] Hence, the problem is not merely that we do not *know* about the preferences of future people. It is not even that we cannot hope to influence *their* preferences. Future generations, taken as wholes, *will not* be mute, deaf, or blind. They *will* be able to learn from our deliberations, from our reasons and from our mistakes. They will even be able to deliberate *among themselves* about them. Yet their current voicelessness prevents them from challenging and potentially transforming *our* preferences, including those with a significant impact on the future. This is the challenge for deliberativists.

Democracy has typically evolved through expanding its circle to voices that were initially muted. When women were finally granted political rights, after centuries of denial and decades of intense fight, male MPs could no longer ignore the actual views of their fellow female MPs. And the political opinions of both male and female MPs became subject to the transformative pressure of deliberation. However, democratic inclusion is not an option for future people. Hence, we can neither gain knowledge about future preferences, nor expose present preferences to the scrutiny of future reasons. The future's *current* "communicative apathy" leaves us with the aftertaste of an offbeat "dialogue." While we may reflect on the future with our own (collective) imagination, this cannot fully replace real collective deliberation held together with future people.[7]

In fact, further clouds are gathering in our sky. I assumed that citizens were exclusively geared toward the common good. Relaxing this assumption allows us to also see democracy as a set of institutions aimed at handling *power relations* between citizens, the latter not being necessarily benevolent toward each other. Democracies handle power in various ways. They distribute it differently depending on a variety of features. The regime can be more presidential or more parliamentary. Separation of power between the legislator, the executive, and the judiciary can vary in rigidity. Citizens may be able to exercise power in a more or less direct manner. Authorization and accountability mechanisms may grant more or less power to citizens to press their representatives.

Yet the future is not only voiceless. It is also (currently) *toothless*.[8] This affects the degree to which we are likely today to effectively act out of benevolence *and* out of fear toward future people. They are unable to authorize or to challenge current decisions today. And politicians who claim to be acting in their name too often take advantage of this, as I stressed in the introduction.[9] While it remains an open question whether the lack of mutual power is good or bad news overall, it certainly limits the range of institutional design options.

I assume here that the present can exercise much more power on the future than the reverse. This *power asymmetry* should of course be qualified. I discuss below the extent to which a generation can be said to *govern* future ones. At this stage, three conclusions may be drawn. *First*, our difficulty in anticipating the preferences of future people and, as a result, aggregating them with ours is a challenge to both intergenerational justice – especially when the metrics is preferentialist – and intergenerational legitimacy. *Second*, while we may shape future preferences to some extent, there is no way in which deliberation can take place beyond the overlap and shape *our* preferences. The preference dynamics is to some extent a one-way story. This means that for democrats attaching a central value to deliberation, future-regarding and perhaps even present-regarding decisions may not be seen as sufficiently legitimate to qualify as intergenerationally democratic. *Third*, power relations are asymmetrical between non-overlapping generations. This raises the question of whether a fair intergenerational balance of powers can be reached at all, and whether decisions can possibly be intergenerationally legitimate in that sense too.

Hence, the difficulties we face with aggregation, deliberative transformation, and a fair balance of powers with the future are structural. They should be duly acknowledged. Of course, one could object that, as for intergenerational justice, what matters is to act in a manner that is *as* intergenerationally legitimate *as possible*. Yet the obstacles may be so serious that they jeopardize our ability to meet the most *minimal* requirements of democratic legitimacy, those without which a decision could not meaningfully be regarded as intergenerationally legitimate. I return to this below.

Government *of* the future?

Let me now approach the matter from another angle. Consider the basic account of democracy as "government *of* the people, *for* the people, *by* the people," in the spirit of Abraham Lincoln's famous 1863 address.[10] Under this "of–for–by" slogan, to qualify as democratic, government of the people should be done for the people *and* by the people. In an evil-minded dictatorship, government *of* the people is done neither *by* the people nor *for* the people. In a benevolent dictatorship, government *of* the people is done *for* the people, yet not *by* the people. Hence, for the "of–for–by" slogan, *intergenerational* democratic legitimacy requires that if we govern several generations, it should be done *for* these several generations and *by* these several generations. At this stage, let us focus on non-overlapping generations. The question that we should keep at the back of our minds is the following: can we do better toward the future than benevolent dictators?

Let me begin with the idea of "government *of* the future." Whether democratic legitimacy requirements toward the future *apply* at all depends on whether we can be said to *govern* the future. Were it not to be the case, it would not mean that we are unable to act *unjustly* toward the future. It would "merely" mean that whatever we do will not be *illegitimate* toward the future. Note the following parallel. In chapter 1, I assessed whether using the concept of harm in a non-identity context immunized our policies from being unjust toward the future. Here, I am evaluating whether relying on the idea of "governing" in a non-overlapping context immunizes our policies from being illegitimate toward the future.

You may understand "governing" in various ways, including more strictly as "ruling the future by law" or more widely as "affecting the future." Picking one interpretation or the other is not without consequences. Our starting point is the view that too wide a notion of "government" may require too large a democratic franchise. This is why limiting us to understanding "governing" as "ruling by law" may seem attractive at first sight. Our question is, then: *can* we rule the future by law, beyond our own lifetime?

It is true that the future will typically inherit a huge body of laws that have piled up over decades or even centuries. It is equally true that we can *try* to render such laws more difficult to modify or repeal through imposing specific revision procedures. It is even true that we can *claim* prescriptive jurisdiction beyond our period of existence, i.e. claim that the future should abide by rule *x* or *y*, as we do among contemporaries with extraterritorial jurisdiction.[11] However, there is no way in which we can prevent future people from repealing our laws after our death. Similarly, we are unable to enforce into the future the laws that our successors would not have formally repealed. In conclusion, if ruling requires the ability to prescribe and enforce a rule, the present cannot be said to rule the future. Note that it is the absence of (physical) coexistence that prevents forward enforcement.

If democratic legitimacy requirements only apply when a group is actually able to rule another, and if the present is actually unable to rule the future, then our actions cannot be democratically illegitimate toward the future. Following this understanding of "ruling the future," the chances of violating the requirements of democratic legitimacy are as low as those arising for a group of people stuck in a room and deciding together that they expect another group stuck in another room to follow a given rule.

Yet this conclusion is troubling. And it may flow from interpreting "governing" too narrowly as "ruling by law."[12] It singles out *one* vehicle through which we exercise power over others. Admittedly, in an *intra*generational setting, this vehicle is potentially quite encompassing. One may claim that all foreigners blocked by country C's anti-immigration laws are actually *ruled* by them.[13] One may claim too that all those who don't violate any laws are also *ruled* by these laws. There is no reason to limit what we label as "the law" to rules that either prohibit or impose behaviors. The law rules a lot in silence, "by default," simply through refraining from using its regulatory power, through neither prohibiting nor imposing myriads of actions. Yet the picture is different in a setting of non-overlapping generations. For all these things that the future will be abstaining from or engaging in *cannot* be loosely described as "ruled by our laws" anymore, simply because the law cannot claim to effectively rule anything in the future, due to our enforcement limitations. Yet our actions may still have a massive impact on the future through other means.

Where do we go from here? We are concerned about how to interpret "governing the future." The future cannot be ruled beyond our existence. If "governing" means "ruling by law," and even if we understand the latter broadly, as we just illustrated, the account of democratic legitimacy captured in the "of–for–by" slogan will *not* trigger demands of legitimacy toward the non-overlapping future. For anyone puzzled by such a conclusion, one alternative is to interpret "governing" more broadly. The "of–for–by" slogan's spirit is that if a state intends to impose a tax on you next year, it should clearly give you a say about it first ("no taxation without representation"). Imagine now a state intending to impose a tax on your as yet unborn children in forty years' time to repay the future interests of a loan contracted today. Why should your children not have a say about it today *if it were possible*? And what would it change that the future state will have the legal option of declaring itself not bound by this foreign loan in the future, if *as a matter of fact* it would threaten its credit to such an extent that it could practically not do it? In the end, how different is it for a future generation that did not participate in enacting a law to abide by this law out of fear of a legal fine, or to be stuck with an inherited contract out of fear of non-legal costs, even if it does not recognize the bindingness of such a contract?

We are imposing burdens on the future, be it through legal liabilities or through depleting resources, building nuclear power plants, setting up time bombs, etc. If democracy is not only about deciding within a range of options predefined by others, but also about defining together what the set of options should be,[14] regardless of whether the latter are framed from legal constraints or not, there should be room for interpreting "governing" more broadly, for instance as "affecting." If so, we can conclude that we *are* governing the future in many ways and that, to that extent, the legitimacy requirements captured in the "of–for–by" slogan *do apply*. This is the position that I will endorse. We now need to find out whether such requirements *can be met*.

Government *for* the future, *by* the future?

The "of–for–by" slogan requires government *for* and *by* the people. The "for the people" requirement certainly excludes evil-intending dictators. It also arguably excludes decisions by strictly self-serving majorities unconcerned about the common good. It even goes beyond the demands of justice, as we may consider democratic decisions that are not primarily driven by the purpose of avoiding injustice. However, the difficulty with "for the people" in the case of future people is their *voicelessness*. Not being able to find out about what future people want renders the "for the future" requirement more generic than it would be among contemporaries. Be that as it may, we can assume that this requirement of the slogan can be met to some extent.

What about the "by the people" requirement in the case of us and the future? While the future's current voicelessness reduces the degree to which we can govern "for the future," it is the future's current toothlessness that makes it impossible to meet the "by the future" requirement. I am not assuming here, conceptually, that true democracy is direct democracy. Nor am I implying, axiologically, that direct democracy is preferable to representative democracy. The "by the people" segment of the slogan could be satisfied through representative forms of democracy in which representatives are accountable to their electorate, through elections or other forms of democratic interactions.

The problem is that when it comes to future people, both the direct and the "representation" avenues seem blocked. Various concepts of representation have been proposed by political theorists.[15] In the context of "representing" future people, representation as trusteeship would arguably make more sense than representation as delegation. Even so, the absence of any plausible form of authorization or accountability between those claiming to represent the future today and future people themselves is a major issue. Similarly, the demands of descriptive representation – as when we ask for women to be represented by at least some women in parliament – cannot be met either. Only current people can speak in the name of future people.

We ought to ask ourselves what purpose is served by labeling some institutions or individuals as *representatives* of those not yet born. These institutions or individuals can of course care about the future, and about how to fairly articulate what we owe to the present and the future. Yet using the notion of representation suggests some special connection, some form of authorization (*ex ante*) or accountability (*ex post*). And while specific accountability schemes have been imagined in relation to the future, they always – and necessarily – involve accountability toward some segment of currently existing people if we intend accountability to have any bite.[16] In addition, while alternative notions of representation have been proposed, they do not rely on processes of authorization or accountability. The question is, then, whether these alternative notions still remain distinct from other notions, such as justice toward the future, for instance.

My take is that, at least out of concern for clarity in public discourse, we should renounce using the notion of "representation of future generations," because none of us can claim to have received any mandate from the future or be accountable to the future in any practical sense. This does not mean that generalist or specialist institutions should not devote energy and expertise to our duties to the future and to how to ensure that they are being fulfilled. It simply means that these institutions should not render their mission unnecessarily mysterious by suggesting some special connection with the future.

If a group of men self-proclaimed or were mandated by other men to *represent* women, and if, for reasons of systematic segregation or due to other radical obstacles to inter-gender communication, they never had any chance to even listen to what women might have to propose or to object, the work of this group of men should not be presented as one of "representing women." For it would not give us a proper sense of what such a group of men *can* reasonably hope and claim to achieve.

Legitimacy *toward* the future?

I have just suggested dropping the notion of representation when it comes to labeling future-oriented institutions. We should not welcome the fact that some segments of the current population, or even the whole current population, vindicate their status as representatives of the future. Again, this does not imply at all that we should not care proactively about the future. It merely means that "representation" mischaracterizes the nature of the relationship that we can hope to entertain with the non-overlapping future. What about *democratic legitimacy* more broadly? Should we also drop expectations of legitimacy toward the future, as we just did for representation?

The answer to this question is complex. I have contrasted one approach claiming that the demands of legitimacy *do not apply* toward the future and another approach that claims that, while applicable, such demands *cannot be met*. Be it due to the present's inability to rule the future or to the future's inability to authorize or to challenge present decisions, democratic legitimacy toward the future of our policies is in doubt in both cases. This leaves us with several avenues. In an "ought implies can" spirit, we may want to conclude that any policy is legitimate toward the future since we cannot rule the future anyway. In contrast, we could also consider our policies as unavoidably "a-legitimate" (rather than the stronger "illegitimate") toward the future. In the latter case, it does not follow that we should do something about it on the legitimacy front. It merely means that "legitimacy toward the future" should not be invoked as a *positive reason* in support of our policies. I am inclined to endorse the latter view. As for the concept of *representation* – and for the phrase *"harming the future"* for another reason – I would renounce using the phrase *"(il)legitimacy toward the future"* altogether.

One might perhaps object that the "of–for–by" slogan does not fully capture what democracy is about. When it comes to non-overlapping generations, we may have to drop any hope of meeting the requirements of a proper demos, of a majority vote covering future people, of any form of deliberation with the future, of any proper representation of the future. And yet we might perhaps have left aside other demands of democracy that *could* be met. Consider separation of powers. I am not referring here to the intergenerational separation of powers resulting from our inability to rule the future by law beyond our death. I am rather referring here to plain separation of power among various institutions within a given period of time. Assuming that some key requirements of a democracy are *not* vulnerable to the effects of the generational gap, would meeting such requirements not be *enough* to characterize our decisions as legitimate toward the future? I doubt it. Consider again our gender-segregated-society analogy. Adding very independent men-only courts in such a society, besides men-only parliamentary chambers and a men-only executive, *would not suffice* to render our policies democratically legitimate toward women. For the same reason, we might have to conclude that we are unable to do better than being benevolent dictators toward the future.

Bleak implications?

Does this leave us with a bleak picture? Not necessarily. It merely means that for the sake of a reasonably intelligible democratic debate, we should avoid using misleading concepts and we should readjust our expectations. It also means that we may have to operate within a more limited conceptual and moral universe when characterizing our duties to the future. Yet dropping the phrase "legitimacy toward the future" still leaves room for at least two types of concerns: legitimacy toward *the present* and *justice* toward the future. Let me spell this out.

It makes perfect sense to ask whether a decision with significant implications for the future meets the demands of democratic decision-making *among contemporaries*. This reflects two types of concerns. On the one hand, citizens don't share the same views about what we owe the future and/or about how to operationalize it. Legitimacy cares here about whether a decision gives due weight to differences in perspectives *among current people* about what we owe the future.

On the other hand, we can be concerned more specifically about whether a decision is legitimate toward the various *generations* that are currently overlapping. The remaining life expectancy varies across coexisting cohorts. This means that a given decision may have different impacts on the various cohorts at stake. I cannot develop here what (if anything) this may entail in terms of institutional design for decisions on pension design, Brexit, or climate change. What matters is that there remains clear room for (il)legitimacy concerns *about* the future and for (il)legitimacy concerns toward *overlapping* generations, even if we drop hopes for legitimacy *toward the future*. Remember as well that the overlap is not only less subject to radical difficulties. It offers again a possible avenue to partly and indirectly handle our duties to the non-overlapping future.

Hence, do the limitations of legitimacy in the non-overlapping context invite us to drop our commitment to *democracy*? The answer is negative. As we said, democratic legitimacy remains meaningful, feasible, and desirable among contemporaries, including across different living generations, independently of its connections with justice. Moreover, transmitting democratic institutions to the future remains a key item in the basket of what we owe the future as a matter of justice. Finally, we might empirically investigate whether a regime that is more democratic among contemporaries today tends to produce decisions that are fairer to the future.[17] In the latter case, democracy among the living is valued as an instrument for justice toward those not yet born. Hence, even if hopes of "legitimacy toward the future" are dropped, democrats should still care about democracy for today, democracy as a good for the future, and democracy as a potential means to deliver justice to the future.

Besides the fact that *intergenerational* legitimacy can still be referred to at the overlap, what follows for intergenerational *justice* – independently of its links with democracy? Justice and legitimacy face less serious challenges at the overlap than beyond. Here, I would add the claim that beyond the overlap, justice faces less serious challenges than legitimacy, for instance if we focus on the sufficientarian component that is less vulnerable to the impossibility of information exchange with the future. If this holds true, the difficulties with legitimacy beyond the overlap invite us to put more emphasis on justice than on democracy when we find ourselves beyond the overlap.

Future-sensitive institutional design

What does dropping hopes of legitimacy toward the future entail for *future-sensitive institutional design*? It stresses the need for lucid institutional design. We have to take seriously the implications of being unable to define future-sensitive policies together with future people. We need to accept the fact that, whatever we do, current policies can only be decided by current people. This invites us to rethink the contribution of institutional design to legitimacy and justice among the living, to solidifying democratic institutions – ensuring that they be delivered alive to the future – and to the promotion of justice toward the future. It may be that, due to the constraints associated with the intergenerational setting, those defending democracy for non-instrumental reasons may have to accept more instrumental defenses when it comes to designing our institutions for a non-overlapping context.

Institutional design concerned about the very long term may well have to renounce the goal of legitimacy toward the future. Yet there remains a wide range of considerations that should be looked at as far as future-oriented institutional design is concerned. What matters here is to stress (and explore) the links between such practical debates and the underlying concerns of justice and legitimacy. Let me list here a few more concrete elements, by way of illustration, of what institutional designers should keep in mind.

First, one should not lose sight of the fact that, if our policies are insufficiently sensitive to the future, it is not merely the outcome of our institutional setting, for instance of the length of electoral cycles. It is also the outcome of substantive policies. If poverty, high uncertainty, or – to the contrary – a feeling of "no future" are key obstacles to projecting ourselves into the future, such features cannot merely be fixed through modifying our decision-making processes.[18] They also require that our *substantive* policies be conceived with an eye on the full range of determinants of short-termism. Our ability to project ourselves into the future is largely endogenous to the content of the decisions we take, not only to the processes through which we take them.

Second, intergenerational justice is not justice biased toward the future. It should care about both the future *and the present*. This is so, not because, in a Hobbesian spirit, it is the present that will have the "last" word. It is so rather because, in a spirit of impartiality, caring about the future should not justify being unfair to the present. And this matters when labeling specific future-oriented institutions and defining their mandate. It is important to understand for each such institution whether its role is one of advocacy in an otherwise imbalanced political environment that systematically ignores the interests of the future, or whether its role requires already balancing the interests of the future and the present, against the background of explicit principles of justice.

Third, as the institutional determinants of problematic short-termism are of various natures, we should also rely on a diverse ecology of institutional instruments, abandoning a "one size fits all" approach. Decision-makers may lack the ability to act in a manner that is future-sensitive enough because they lack *knowledge* about the future, because they lack *jurisdiction* within the existing institutional ecosystem, or because they simply lack the *incentives* (or the intrinsic motivation) to do so. If the determinant of short-termism is not unique, we may have to rely on a set of separate institutions.[19] For instance, if we value independent fact-finding about the future, this may have to be done by institutions that are independent from decision-makers, no matter how future-sensitive we manage to render the latter. Similarly, lengthening mandates may both increase our temporal jurisdiction and weaken accountability mechanisms, as the group to which we are accountable will less frequently have a say, including about whether our policies are future-sensitive enough. Hence, when we render central banks independent to insulate monetary policy from short electoral cycles, we may still want to pay attention to the fact that reducing the accountability of central banks may also put them under less pressure to be sensitive to future interests.

As well, it may make sense to increase the future-sensitivity of our decision-making processes by adding *specialized* institutions when needed. For instance, the IPCC is a model that could inspire a specialist institution focusing on the broader future impacts of our decisions. And watchdogs such as ombudspersons or commissioners for future generations have been and are still being experimented with in various countries.[20] Yet, besides specialist institutions, it seems even more important to reinforce or reform some of our generalist institutions to guarantee their future-sensitivity, building on empirical evidence.

For instance, stressing the toothlessness of future people invites us to reinforce the degree to which our societies are ruled by principles rather than by power relations, which may be a challenge for accounts of democracy that give a central role to conflict. One way in which this can be done consists in guaranteeing the independence of the judiciary and its ability to check whether our policies are up to the demands of the laws and constitutional provisions that we adopted ourselves. Separation of powers may encourage more principle-driven policies. And more principle-driven policies may in turn be associated with more impartial policy making, which may mean more justice, including toward the future. Similarly, we can also explore the degree to which more direct or more deliberative forms of democracy may encourage more future-sensitive decision-making.[21]

Besides insisting on reinforcing the future-sensitivity of generalist institutions rather than putting all the emphasis on specialized future-focused institutions, we may also want to reinforce the ability of our institutions to draw on the multigenerational nature *of the living population* as an opportunity to put us on the right track toward the non-living. This indirect (yet intergenerational) path toward the future is a strategy that has been popping up here and there all along the book. The burgeoning public-interest litigation about climate change is a case in point. Not only does it illustrate the importance of an independent judiciary for future-sensitive policy; it also illustrates the interests of drawing on the multigenerational nature of our constituencies to try to handle the effects of current policies on the relatively remote future. Some plaintiffs in such cases are very young, with an additional life expectancy that can extend more than fifty years ahead. This allows us to force current decision-makers to care about the future effects of some of our current policies on already existing people.

There is some margin for change in our institutional design. Yet we should remain lucid about what can be reasonably hoped for. The inclusion of women in formerly men-dominated decision-making processes has led to significant progresses in gender justice. Yet, after decades of inclusion, major gender injustices still remain. And what we can hope for with respect to future-sensitivity is much more limited, as the inclusion of future people is not an option. Being lucid about what can be hoped for on the side of institutional design may prevent us from losing sight of where the emphasis should be put in priority when caring about the future.

Conclusion

We probably need to drop claims of *representing* the future or hopes to design our institutions to achieve democratic legitimacy *toward the future*. The problem is not that demands of legitimacy are *inapplicable* because we cannot "rule the future by law." The issue is rather that *we* cannot be governed by the future. The latter can neither authorize policies that we would adopt in their name, nor hold us accountable for such policies while we are alive. This is the core issue.

While dropping hopes for legitimacy *toward* the non-overlapping future forces us to significantly readjust our expectations, it is far from closing the door to any concern about our duties to the future. It still leaves room for concerns about legitimacy toward our contemporaries – including of different generations – whenever we deal with policies of significant future impact. It also leaves ample room for concerns of justice toward non-overlapping future generations, even if preferentialism confronts us with serious difficulties. It still preserves the importance of democracy for the future. And it also leaves space for future-sensitive options for institutional design with a lucid understanding of its feasible and desirable purpose.

Hence, the limitations we encounter with representation and legitimacy should not make us feel lighter about the future. They merely invite us to properly characterize the nature of what should be expected from us regarding the future, and to put the right labels on our policy proposals to ensure both their intelligibility by our citizens and their chances of reaching goals that are actually reachable.

Conclusion

After having set the stage, I devoted a chapter to the non-identity problem. I stressed the extensive nature of this challenge. It touches not only on issues of substantive duties to the future, but also on issues of legitimate coercion or on duties to the past, not to mention key issues in bioethics. I explored three core strategies to address the challenge. One – relatively frequent – relies on an alternative understanding of the concept of harm. Another – less common – builds on the possibility of limiting the challenge's scope to part of the intergenerational overlap. And the third – labeled "severance," and what I consider the most promising one – insists on the relationship between harm and distributive duties. It stresses that our duties may be understood to a significant extent without invoking the notion of harm. I also alluded to a fourth "indirect" strategy that came back in our discussion on sustainability.

Chapter 2 contrasted four ways of understanding our duties to the future at the level of principles, framed in the Rawlsian language of generational savings and dis-savings. I ended up insisting on the leximin egalitarian approach

– which I referred to as "narrow path" – and on what I consider to be one of the core challenges to any theory of intergenerational justice: how to justify the authorization to transfer to the next generation *more* than we inherited? I then moved further in two directions. I showed why framing such issues in "savings" and "dis-savings" terms tends to invite us to consider what we inherit from the previous generation as a standard rather than as a constraint. Dropping the exclusive focus on inheritance opens the gate to reframing the four views in an alternative language. It invites us to think more explicitly about what else, other than inheritance, can contribute to what we transfer to the future. It also allows us to see how different the reciprocity-based "non-decline" and the sufficientarian "having enough" accounts turn out to be.

This leads us to the other direction that I explored in combination with principles of intergenerational justice: sustainability. The latter typically comes in a "non-decline" or a "having enough" version. Building on seminal work by Brian Barry, I explored whether sustainability is sufficient and necessary for meeting the demands of intergenerational justice. In the end, the structure in three steps of chapter 2 allows us to see not only the diversity of options within a savings/dis-savings language, but also the promises of dropping that language and the complexity of the justice–sustainability nexus. While far from fixing all the issues raised, this offers us some starting points to make up our mind about what we owe the future, through a reflective equilibrium exercise.

Yet defending precise principles of justice to the future without giving a sense of our currency of justice would be pointless. I devoted chapter 3 to giving this sense. The picture I explored is twofold. I pointed to the difference between a more "objective" metrics and a more "preference-based" one. I stressed the reasons why sufficientarians may want to adopt metrics of the "basic needs" or "basic capabilities" type. I then devoted most of the chapter to the difficulties faced by more "preference-based" metrics, Dworkinian resourcism being one of them. Such a currency can be used to handle demands that go beyond sufficiency, for example those of a leximin egalitarian nature. There are challenges both from a static and from a dynamic perspective, depending on whether we take future preferences as exogenous or take into account the fact that what we do influences those future preferences. In the latter case, challenges occur beyond but also within the overlap. They have to do with how our ways of life and our education programs contribute to forming the preferences of the next generation(s).

I explored three possible proposals: focusing on intangible heritage, keeping options open, and privileging frugality. There is no simple takeaway message. What matters is to understand what the underlying intuitions and challenges are in each case and how they connect with a general metrics – such as "resources" in the Dworkinian sense. One of the ideas that I stressed is the role of education in preserving a gap between exposure and aspirations. I also made some tentative claims about issues of "substitutability." Typically discussed in the sustainability literature, they are central to testing currencies of intergenerational justice as well.

In the end, the intergenerational setting confronts us with a situation in which we have less knowledge about the preferences of future people and perhaps more control over such preferences through exposure and education than we do with contemporaries. The difficulty is to stick in such a context to some neutrality toward the various conceptions of the good life, while not ending up with "anything goes" types of conclusions, be it through excessive techno-optimism or through claims such as "No worries about environmental degradation! We will ensure that future preferences adjust."

Chapter 4 moved to illustrating the possible implications of the previous chapters for the core environmental challenge of our times: climate change. I looked into the significance of historical emissions for climate justice in general and for our obligations to the future in particular. I advocated a forward-looking, distributive approach, distinguishing three ways of understanding the demands of distributive climate justice. I also stressed that even a charitable look at different provisos ends up in trouble when it comes to justifying intergenerationally the 2°C degradation of our global climate. Early effort is another intergenerational issue that I looked at, exploring three different ways of justifying it. Finally, we had a closer look at the social discount rate debate. On these four issues of intergenerational climate justice, we can clearly see the relevance of a general theory of justice, for instance when contrasting different understandings of climate justice, or when considering the relevance of "narrow path" in approaching the early-effort issue. At the same time, we always need to keep an eye on the extra complexity brought by the focus on a specific domain.

In the final chapter, I looked at issues of democratic legitimacy beyond the overlap. The key message is that both the voicelessness and the toothlessness of future people invite us to readjust what democrats can hope for in terms of legitimacy. Admittedly, democratic requirements do not limit themselves to inclusion and accountability. Yet it is reasonable to consider that beyond the overlap, the conditions are not met to claim that a decision that would comply with all the demands of democracy that *can* be complied with in such a setting would meet the minimum demands of democratic legitimacy. The lack of accountability or the impossibility of deliberation are such that we should just renounce using notions such as "representing the future" or "legitimacy toward the future." What matters is that this still leaves room for concerns of legitimacy of decision-making among contemporaries about the future, and for concerns of justice to the future. It also leaves plenty of room for evidence-based and creative institutional design. The latter can be valuable if it properly understands what it is unreasonable to hope for, given the structural limitations of a non-overlapping setting.

* * *

Because of space limitations, I have had to leave aside many important issues, for instance demographic ones.[1] Let me come back, however, to some worries that may still subsist in the reader's mind at this stage. Readers might have the feeling that philosophers overstate the importance of the "overlap/non-overlap" distinction, as economists may overstate the importance of the "finite/infinite horizon" distinction in an intergenerational setting.[2] There is no doubt that the issue of coexistence is central to intergenerational relations. It turned out to play a central role in each and every chapter of this book. In the introduction, I insisted on the need to properly articulate it with the "age group/birth cohort" distinction. In chapter 1, the overlap was central in the second strategy aimed at addressing the non-identity problem. In chapter 3, the absence of overlap was seen as a major problem for preferentialists. In chapter 4, the whole issue of historical emissions was about whether one should be held responsible for the consequences of actions by groups or individuals with which we never coexisted. In chapter 5, coexistence turned out to be central to the debate on whether we can rule the future, to the possibility of aggregating and deliberating about preferences, and to power relations in a democracy.

While the overlap/non-overlap distinction is essential to understand the anatomy of intergenerational relations, philosophically significant issues also arise within the overlap. The latter is central to justice between age groups, a dimension that we only alluded to. The non-identity problem arises between both overlapping and non-overlapping persons. Most of the issues discussed in chapter 2 arise in an overlapping context as well. As to the metrics dimension, the issue of preference dynamics does not disappear once we move to an overlapping setting. For climate change, while the absence of overlap was central to the discussion on historical emissions, the questions about the justifiability of climate degradation or of early effort clearly arise in an overlapping setting. And regarding legitimacy, Brexit is a good illustration of issues of legitimacy of decision-making processes involving several coexisting generations.

Hence, non-coexistence is definitely a central difference-maker of intergenerational relations. Yet one ought to understand what does not follow from this claim. First, it does not follow that we should only focus on the relationships between generations that will *never* coexist. The overlap refers to a situation in which we only coexist during *part* of our lives. And this as such is a source of challenges and possibilities. While this is magnified in an intergenerational setting, it can also occur within a single generation, for instance between the short-lived and long-lived members of a birth cohort that will only coexist during part of their life.

Second, it does not follow that *non-coexistence* is the *only* difference-maker of intergenerational relations. There are other important features. There is the one-directionality of time (time's arrow) and the information or power asymmetries associated with it. There is also the fact that the unique link between the cohortal and the age dimensions is such that we begin and end our coexistence with neighboring generations in a state of vulnerability (age dependency). Another important fact is that one cohort is causally responsible through reproduction for the very existence of the next one, and to some degree for its size. I cannot unfold here the full anatomy of intergenerational relations and explore the normative implications of each of its features. Some of the features may not even be unique to intergenerational relations. But what matters is that they are central to the latter and that they combine in a unique manner.

Other aspects of the book may possibly have puzzled the readers too. For instance, they may be under the impression that it does not reflect well enough a concern for the *global poor*. This sense could emerge, for instance, from reading my arguments on historical emissions. However, I stressed in the introduction how I see the connection between intergenerational and global justice. And it emerged again in the discussion of possible accounts of distributive climate justice. To my eyes, the demands of global justice are crucial, especially in such a massively unjust world as ours. Yet it matters to me that the nature of such demands be expressed in the most philosophically robust manner, even if this may force me to depart from more widespread views, for instance about historical injustice. And of course, since the focus was on the intergenerational dimension, I could not devote space to some of the central issues of global justice, such as the role of the extractive industry, the desirability of open borders, the assessment of free trade, or the absence of any significant global redistribution mechanisms.

The whole argument may also have seemed *too liberal*, in the philosophical sense, leading to unnecessarily impoverished claims about what matters tremendously to many of us, be it the beauty of a cork oak savanna or the sense of Caucasian hospitality.[3] I am not assuming here that reasons flowing from specific conceptions of the good life are not worth articulating and defending philosophically. I believe, though, that for the purposes of political philosophy (as opposed to ethics in general), there is a strong case for aiming at some form of neutrality toward the variety of conceptions of the good life, including in an intergenerational context. This is so because what is at stake is the imposition of rules on others. It may well be that this liberal account to some degree fails or faces too-significant limitations, especially in handling situations in which the preferences of others are unknown or in which their preferences are under our own control during at least the initial part of their life. But I have tried at least to articulate what such an account would allow us to defend.

Finally, despite my initial words of caution, this book might still leave the most action-oriented readers among us frustrated. The purpose was to provide those who do not devote all their time to the philosophical dimensions of intergenerational justice with a sense of the nature and depth of those questions, a sketch of possible arguments, and an indication of those that I find the most convincing. I believe that this should at least help activists to reflect on whether they are defending the right cause in the name of intergenerational justice, to think about the degree to which their arguments can support what they are fighting for, and to even consider the views of their opponents with the necessary charity, without necessarily lowering their level of commitment. Our world needs radical changes. And I think that philosophical reflection on intergenerational issues can contribute to it. This is why I wrote this book.

Notes

Introduction

1 Rawls (1971), Barry and Sikora (1978), Parfit (1984), Heyd (1992), Laslett and Fishkin (1992), Gosseries and Meyer (2009), just to mention a few.
2 Fleurbaey and Blanchet (2013).
3 See Kohli (2005: 518), White (2013: 231), Baker (2018), Moury (2018), Chauvel and Schröder (2014), Chauvel (2019), Hillier (2019).
4 Fleurbaey (2005).
5 See Vandeschrick (2001).
6 See Landes (2015).
7 Daniels (1988), McKerlie (2012), Gosseries (2014a), Uhuru Bidadanure (2021).
8 Gal, Vanhuysse, and Vargha (2018).
9 I leave aside further challenges. For instance, the neo-Hobbesian account of justice is sensitive to the conditions under which individuals are likely to *accept* subjecting themselves to a joint authority. Hence, it approaches enforceability differently from e.g. libertarianism. Neo-Hobbesians insist on the mutuality of the benefits of cooperation and on the credibility of mutual threats, which renders justice between non-overlapping generations harder to defend. For an unsuccessful attempt: Heath (2013).

Chapter One

1 See e.g. Parfit (1976), (1984), Woodward (1986), Heyd (1992), Roberts (1998), Shiffrin (1999), Gosseries (2004a), Boonin (2014).

2 See also the stylized examples of Parfit (1984) and Boonin (2014).

3 Broome (2012: 63): "The compensation and the non-identity argument constitute a case for doubting that injustice is done to future generations."

4 E.g. D. W. Brock (1998).

5 E.g. Bognar (2016).

6 The non-identity context is not the only challenge to the comparative-to-counterfactual concept of harm. When facing an allegedly harmful act, one could argue in many cases that had this act not taken place, the victim would have found herself in exactly *the same* situation (e.g. because the abstaining actor would have been immediately replaced by a competitor doing exactly the same), or even in a *worse* one (e.g. when missing your plane because of a too-slow taxi driver actually preserves you from a plane crash). See e.g. Bradley (2012), Johansson and Risberg (2019).

7 Gosseries (2004a: 54).

8 For an introduction to this debate: Luper (2021).

9 See Holtug (2002), Endörfer (2021) (on Mill's harm principle and market harms).

10 For a first approach: Brink (2018: sect. 3.6).

11 Thanks to J. Nedevska for drawing my attention to this.

12 Scheffler (2018).

13 There are even cases in which, while an injustice obtains, no one has an obligation to do something about it today. See Gosseries (2019) (unjust inequalities between us and the past).

14 On the relationship between harm, interests, and rights violations: Feinberg (1984).

15 Endörfer (2021).

16 On how to articulate corrective and distributive justice: Perry (2000), Cohen (2016).

17 See Fabre (2008).

18 I leave aside e.g. the issue of whether duties of relational justice matter more than those of distributive justice.

19 For a critical discussion: Risse (2005).

20 I am indebted to an external referee for pressing me on this.

21 On harm-based responses to wrongful life situations from the angles of meaningfulness, completeness, and fairness: Gosseries (2004a).

22 I assume here that *pro tanto* wrongs should be rejected as an option. They would entail the possibility of wrongs without anyone having "wronged" anyone, all things considered. While we may have *pro tanto reasons* to act in one way or another, I think that *duties* should only be affirmed as the outcome of an all-things-considered reasoning. One ought to reject the idea of *pro tanto* duties.

23 This account presupposes the rejection of the compossibility of rights requirement.

24 In wrongful life cases, relying on a life-worth-living threshold concept of harm potentially raises two extra difficulties, if we use it to go for a tort-based – as opposed to a social-security-based – solution to address the difficulties faced by children disabled to the point of dragging them below the life-worth-living threshold. First, two children with the same disability will receive different benefits depending on whether their existence was affected or not by a mistaken preconception advisory opinion provided by a medical practitioner. Second, expecting the medical doctor who provided the mistaken diagnosis to cover alone the costs associated with a disability that results itself from a fact of nature is unfairly burdensome to a single individual, who, after all, did not generate the disability itself. See Gosseries (2004a).

25 We could propose a *probabilistic* adjustment of the life-not-worth-living standard: a person would be "harmed" if we significantly increased the *risk* of her falling below the harm threshold. While this would widen the proposal's scope, I do not think it would suffice to address the challenge.

26 What about a one-shot assessment at the age of e.g. sixty? Leaving aside the problem of those who do not make it to sixty, it would mean that whatever happens in terms of transmission and destruction between sixty and the duty-holder's death does not count. Hence, this option is unattractive: we could wipe off all that we have accumulated until sixty without acting unfairly to the next generation, as long as it is done after the age of sixty.

27 I owe this extended overlap idea to Claus Offe, who owes it to Max Frisch.
28 On chains and generations: Howarth (1992), Gosseries (2022).
29 On this distinction: Gosseries (2004a).
30 Moreover, we will see in ch. 2 that if some of our intergenerational obligations, e.g. the obligation not to transfer too much to the next generation, can be interpreted primarily as obligations toward some the members of *our own generation*, this too won't be subject to the non-identity problem.

Chapter Two

1 See Rawls (1971: §44, "just savings principle").
2 On intergenerational reciprocity: Barry (1989), Wade-Benzoni (2002), Gosseries (2009).
3 A reciprocity-based view could allow for net transfers if it relied on an endowment-sensitive, effort-based metrics that takes disadvantage into account. This would, however, amount to moving away from the core reciprocity intuition.
4 It would do so for reasons that differ from the one stressed in the "narrow path" view (below).
5 Non-utilitarian reasons may also support an accumulation phase. For instance, Rawls justifies an accumulation phase by the need to reach the level of wealth needed to support just institutions. On Rawls's "institutionalist sufficientarianism": Gaspart and Gosseries (2007), Gosseries (2014b). In addition, the "narrow path" view can also impose compulsory savings, e.g. in cases of predictable exogenous future catastrophe. I assume here that utilitarianism is the most at home with the idea of compulsory generational savings.
6 Worsening factors include the indefinite number of future generations as well as – to a more limited degree – the existence of descending altruism. Additional attenuating factors include diminishing marginal utility and the possibility of discounting on grounds of uncertainty. See ch. 4 on the latter.
7 Broome and Foley (2016).
8 On sufficientarianism: Casal (2007), Gosseries (2011), Shields (2016). On intergenerational sufficientarianism: Meyer and Roser (2009), Gosseries (2016).

9 See Solow (1974), Gaspart and Gosseries (2007). Also Cohen (2008: v).
10 Van Parijs (2001).
11 See, however, Loi (2014).
12 Gini prioritarianism aims at maximizing a weighted average. Weights depend on ranks. In a two-individuals world, and taking income as a reference, a ¼ weight will be assigned to an additional unit of income to the richest individual while the weight of an additional unit to the poorest one is ¾. I am indebted to F. Maniquet on this. On prioritarianism, see for example: Adler and Norheim (2022).
13 Rawls (1971: §4).
14 I leave aside here the extra complication of whether the sufficiency threshold should adjust upward over time.
15 See e.g. Scheffler (2018).
16 See Barry (1997), Goodin (1999).
17 Barry (1997: 45): "Is sustainability (however we understand the term) either a necessary or a sufficient condition of inter-generational distributive justice?"
18 Rey (2012: 1190).
19 Asheim (2010: 206).
20 Barry (1997: 50).
21 WCED (1987: 53). See also Gosseries (2016), including on an earlier definition by Pinchot.
22 See Barry (1997: 54): "the root idea of sustainability is the *conservation of what matters to future generations*" (my emphasis).
23 See Howarth (1992: 134) ("we are harming our children by compromising their ability to fulfil their moral obligations while maintaining a favourable way of life for themselves. A generalization of this argument … shows that the responsibility of one generation to provide for the next defines a chain of obligation that extends into the indefinite future"); Gosseries (2004a: 97–100) ("transitivity strategy"); Gheaus (2016: 499)("Given the generational overlap, this model takes us all the way to a duty of sustainability. I showed why *G1*'s duty to give adequate life prospects to *G2* includes a duty to give them enough to sustain an adequate life for *G3*. Since members of *G3* will also have a fundamental interest in rearing children, if *G1* does not leave enough for a potential *G4*, then G1 forces on *G2* the following choice:

either some members of *G2* forgo their right to parent adequately ..., or else *G2* has children (the members of *G3*) some of whom it places in the position to choose between remaining childless or else having children (the members of *G4*) for whom it cannot provide adequately. ... The reasoning goes on, justifying the same duty for an indefinite number of generations.")

24 See also the relevance of the "negative/positive duties" distinction for our second strategy to address the implications of the non-identity problem (ch. 1).

25 See Gheaus (2015). Contra: Kaczmarek and Beard (2020).

Chapter Three

1 See Chalmers (2022).
2 See the sources cited in ch. 2, note 8.
3 On basic needs and basic capabilities: Sen (1992), G. Brock (1998), Nussbaum (2011), Robeyns (2017). On metrics in the intergenerational context: Page (2007), Lippert-Rasmussen (2012a).
4 Dworkin (1981).
5 Dworkin (1981: 288).
6 Dutton, van der Linden, and Lynn (2016).
7 Rawls (1971: §15).
8 Brand (2009).
9 Here, I am *not* talking about rendering some *principles* binding, e.g. through relying on constitutional rigidity. See Gosseries (2014c), (2021).
10 Brown Weiss (1990: 202) (principle of "conservation of options"); Feinberg (1992).
11 See Kahn (1999).
12 See Lotz (2006: 546ff).
13 See Lotz (2006: 546) (diff. maximally diverse).
14 For a related discussion: Cohen (2012).
15 Gosseries (2014c).
16 Gardiner (2011a: 153–4).
17 Easterlin and O'Connor (2020).
18 On structuralist vs. voluntarist approaches on the matter: Zwarthoed (2015: 288).
19 Lippert-Rasmussen (2012a: 510).
20 See Zwarthoed (2015: 296).
21 See Zwarthoed (2015: 298–301).

22 I am indebted to Anca Gheaus for pressing me on this.
23 Lotz (2006: 541) (notion of "approximated neutrality"). See also Mills (2003), Millum (2014).
24 Lippert-Rasmussen (2012a: 511).
25 Lippert-Rasmussen (2012a: 511). I am leaving aside here the possibility that leading frugal lives may actually encourage others to lead less frugal lives, be it as a child-vs.-parents reaction, or through market-induced rebound effects on resource prices. See Zwarthoed (2015: 292).
26 Neumayer (2003).
27 Wilson (2016).
28 See Gardiner (2011a: 263).

Chapter Four
1 See Gosseries and Zwarthoed (2016).
2 Garvey (2008: 77–8) (did not know/did not intend); Miller (2009: 130ff) (discussion on harmfulness); Risse (2012: 198–201) (blameless wrong).
3 On historical responsibility in general: Butt (2006), Meyer (2021); on responsibility for historical emissions: Neumayer (2000), Gosseries (2004b), Meyer (2004), Caney (2005), Miller (2009), Page (2012).
4 I leave aside the morally tricky "intergenerational deterrence" justification of holding descendants responsible for the acts of their ancestors.
5 See, however, Page (2012).
6 See Shue (2022).
7 See O'Neill and O'Neill (2012).
8 On time-locked generations: Gosseries (2022).
9 For a critique: Posner and Weisbach (2010).
10 See Caney (2012).
11 Knutti et al. (2015: 17).
12 Jordan et al. (2013), Knutti et al. (2015: 14).
13 Knutti et al. (2015).
14 Randalls (2010).
15 See Sagoff (1988) for a critique.
16 Stern (2007).
17 Gardiner (2011a: 153).
18 Compare with Broome and Foley (2016).
19 There is an ongoing debate among (climate) economists on the social discount rate: e.g. Broome (1992: ch. 3), Nordhaus

(2007), Stern (2007), Dasgupta (2011), Roemer (2011: sect. 2–3), Asheim (2012). The issue is also extensively discussed by philosophers: e.g. Rawls (1971: §45), Cowen and Parfit (1992), Caney (2009), Moellendorf (2014: 99–122). See as well Frederick (2003).

20 Ramsey (1928: 261) ("it is assumed [in the model] that we do not discount later enjoyments in comparison with earlier ones, a practice which is ethically indefensible ...; we shall, however, in Sect. 2, include a rate of discount in some of our investigations").

21 Broome (2008: 71).

22 One of the issues that I have left aside here is that of "termination shock," discussed in the geoengineering literature. See e.g. McKinnon (2019).

Chapter Five

1 See Jacobs (2011), Gonzalez-Ricoy and Gosseries (2016a), Boston (2017), Caney (2019), Gonzalez-Ricoy (2020), Smith (2020), (2021), MacKenzie (2021).

2 On a distinct challenge for the existence and actionability of rights of future people: Gosseries (2008).

3 Christiano and Bajaj (2022).

4 See Lippert-Rasmussen (2012b): critically exploring E. Anderson's democratic egalitarianism.

5 Goodin (2007).

6 Elster (1986).

7 See Goodin (2000: 98) ("communicative inertia"), (2000: 84, 99ff, 109) (on the incomplete substitutability of "external-collective" deliberation with "internal-reflective" deliberation).

8 Here, we only look at the connection between toothlessness and democracy. Some theories of justice also care about toothlessness. Non-coexistence is key to some contractarian theories of justice. In a Hobbesian spirit ascribing a central role to mutual advantage, the very existence of duties of justice may depend on the possibility of credible and *mutual* threats between potential right-holders. The credibility and mutuality of such threats arguably require coexistence.

9 See also Karnein (2016: sect. 5.2.3).

10 The order of Lincoln's original phrase ("of ..., by ..., for ... ") has been adjusted to the sequence of my argument.

11 See Gosseries (2021).
12 See also Rose (2019: 42–4).
13 See Gosseries (2021).
14 Thanks to L. Beckman for pressing me on this.
15 Karnein (2016).
16 Gonzalez-Ricoy and Gosseries (2016b).
17 See e.g. Ward (2008), Bättig and Bernauer (2009), Wurster (2013), Povitkina (2018), Fairbrother et al. (2021).
18 See Slemrod (1986), MacKenzie (2016), Caney (2019).
19 Gonzalez-Ricoy and Gosseries (2016b), MacKenzie (2016).
20 E.g. Koskimaa and Raunio (2020), Smith (2021).
21 E.g. MacKenzie (2021).

Conclusion
1 E.g. Arrhenius, Budolfson, and Spears (2021).
2 Diamond (1965).
3 For a related discussion: Jamieson (2010), Gardiner (2011b).

References

Adler, M. and O. Norheim (eds.), 2022. *Prioritarianism in Practice*, Cambridge: Cambridge University Press.

Arrhenius, G., M. Budolfson, and D. Spears, 2021. "Does Climate Change Policy Depend Importantly on Population Ethics?" in M. Budolfson, T. McPherson, and D. Plunkett (eds.), *Philosophy and Climate Change*, Oxford: Oxford University Press.

Asheim, G., 2010. "Intergenerational Equity," *Annual Review of Economics* 2: 197–222.

Asheim, G., 2012. "Discounting while Treating Generations Equally," in R. W. Hahn and A. Ulph (eds.), *Climate Change and Common Sense: Essays in Honour of Tom Schelling*, Oxford/New York: Oxford University Press.

Baker, D., 2018. "Diverting Class War into Generational War, Again," *Counterpunch*, Oct. 31.

Barry, B., 1989. "Justice as Reciprocity," in *Liberty and Justice*, Oxford: Oxford University Press.

Barry, B., 1997. "Sustainability and Intergenerational Justice," *Theoria* 89: 43–64.

Barry, B. and R. Sikora (eds.), 1978. *Obligations to Future Generations*, Philadelphia: Temple University Press.

Bättig, M. and T. Bernauer, 2009. "National Institutions and Global Public Goods: Are Democracies More Cooperative in Climate Change Policy?" *International Organization* 63: 281–308.

Bognar, G., 2016. "Is Disability Mere Difference?" *Journal of Medical Ethics* 42(1): 46–9.

Boonin, D., 2014. *The Non-Identity Problem and the Ethics of Future People*, New York: Oxford University Press.

Boston, J., 2017. *Governing for the Future: Designing Democratic Institutions for a Better Tomorrow*, Bingley: Emerald.

Bradley, B., 2012. "Doing Away with Harm," *Philosophy and Phenomenological Research* 85(2): 390–412.

Brand, F., 2009. "Critical Natural Capital Revisited: Ecological Resilience and Sustainable Development," *Ecological Economics* 68(3): 605–12.

Brink, D., 2018. "Mill's Moral and Political Philosophy," *The Stanford Encyclopedia of Philosophy* (Winter 2018 edn.), E. N. Zalta (ed.), <https://plato.stanford.edu/archives/win2018/entries/mill-moral-political/>.

Brock, D. W., 1998. "Cloning Human Beings: An Assessment of the Ethical Issues Pro and Con," in M. C. Nussbaum and C. R. Sunstein (eds.), *Facts and Fantasies about Human Cloning*, New York: Norton.

Brock, G. (ed.), 1998. *Necessary Goods: Our Responsibilities to Meet Others' Needs*, Oxford: Rowman and Littlefield.

Broome, J., 1992. *Counting the Cost of Global Warming*, Cambridge/Isle of Harris: White Horse Press.

Broome, J., 2008. "The Ethics of Climate Change," *Scientific American* 198(6): 69–73.

Broome, J., 2012. *Climate Matters: Ethics in a Warming World*, New York and London: Norton.

Broome, J. and D. Foley, 2016. "A World Climate Bank," in I. Gonzalez-Ricoy and A. Gosseries (eds.), *Institutions for Future Generations*, Oxford: Oxford University Press.

Brown Weiss, E., 1990. "Our Rights and Obligations to Future Generations for the Environment," *American Journal of International Law* 84: 198–207.

Butt, D., 2006. "Nations, Overlapping Generations and Historic Injustice," *American Philosophical Quarterly* 43(4): 357–67.

Caney, S., 2005. "Cosmopolitan Justice, Responsibility and Global Climate Change," *Leiden Journal of International Law* 18: 747–75.

Caney, S., 2009. "Climate Change and the Future: Discounting for Time, Wealth, and Risk," *Journal of Social Philosophy* 40(2): 163–86.

Caney, S., 2012. "Just Emissions," *Philosophy and Public Affairs* 40(4): 255–300.

Caney, S., 2019. *Democratic Reform, Intergenerational Justice and the Challenges of the Long-Term*, CUSP Essay Series on the Morality of Sustainable Prosperity.

Casal, P., 2007. "Why Sufficiency is Not Enough," *Ethics* 117(2): 296–326.

Chalmers, D. 2022. *Reality+: Virtual Worlds and the Problems of Philosophy*, New York/Oxford: Oxford University Press.

Chauvel, L. 2019. *La Spirale du Déclassement: Les Désillusions des Classes Moyennes*, Paris: Points.

Chauvel, L. and M. Schröder, 2014. "Generational Inequalities and Welfare Regimes," *Social Forces* 92(4): 1259–83.

Christiano, T. and S. Bajaj, 2022. "Democracy," *The Stanford Encyclopedia of Philosophy* (Spring 2022 edn.), E. N. Zalta (ed.), <https://plato.stanford.edu/archives/spr2022/entries/democracy/>.

Cohen, A., 2016. "Corrective vs. Distributive Justice: The Case of Apologies," *Ethical Theory and Moral Practice* 19: 663–77.

Cohen, G. A., 2008. "Peter Mew on Justice and Capitalism," *Inquiry* 29: 315–323.

Cohen, G. A., 2012. "Rescuing Conservatism: A Defense of Existing Value," in *Finding Oneself in the Other*, Princeton: Princeton University Press.

Cowen, T. and D. Parfit, 1992. "Against the Social Discount Rate," in P. Laslett and J. Fishkin (eds.), *Justice between Age Groups and Generations*, New Haven/London: Yale University Press.

Daniels, N., 1988. *Am I My Parent's Keeper? An Essay on Justice Between the Young and the Old*, New York/Oxford: Oxford University Press.

Dasgupta, P., 2011. "The Ethics of Intergenerational Distribution: Reply and Response to John E. Roemer," *Environmental and Resource Economics* 50(4): 475–93.

Diamond, P., 1965. "The Evaluation of Infinite Utility Streams," *Econometrica* 33(1): 170–7.

Dutton, E., D. van der Linden, and R. Lynn, 2016. "The Negative Flynn Effect: A Systematic Literature Review," *Intelligence* 59: 163–9.

Dworkin, R., 1981. "What is Equality? Part 2: Equality of Resources," *Philosophy and Public Affairs* 10: 283–345.

Easterlin, R. and K. O'Connor, 2020. *The Easterlin Paradox.* IZA Discussion Paper No. 13923, <https://ssrn.com/abstract =3743147>.

Elster, J., 1986. "The Market and the Forum: Three Varieties of Political Theory," in J. Elster and A. Hyllund (eds.), *Foundations of Social Choice Theory*, Cambridge: Cambridge University Press.

Endörfer, R., 2021. "Should Market Harms be an Exception to the Harm Principle?" *Economics and Philosophy* 38(2): 221–41.

Fabre, C. 2008. *Whose Body is it Anyway? Justice and the Integrity of the Person*, Oxford: Oxford University Press.

Fairbrother, M., G. Arrhenius, K. Bykvist, and T. Campbell, 2021. "Governing for Future Generations: How Political Trust Shapes Attitudes towards Climate and Debt Policies," *Frontiers in Political Science* (3): 656053.

Feinberg, J., 1984. *Harm to Others: The Moral Limits of the Criminal Law*, Oxford: Oxford University Press.

Feinberg, J., 1992. "The Child's Right to an Open Future," in *Freedom and Fulfillment: Philosophical Essays*, Princeton: Princeton University Press.

Fleurbaey, M, 2005. "Freedom with Forgiveness," *Politics, Philosophy and Economics* 4(1): 26–67.

Fleurbaey, M. and P. Blanchet, 2013. *Beyond GDP: Measuring Welfare and Assessing Sustainability*, Oxford: Oxford University Press.

Frederick, S., 2003. "Measuring Intergenerational Time Preference: Are Future Lives Valued Less?" *Journal of Risk and Uncertainty* 26(1): 39–53.

Gal, R., P. Vanhuysse, and L. Vargha, 2018. "Pro-Elderly Welfare States within Child-Oriented Societies," *Journal of European Public Policy* 25(6): 944–58.

Gardiner, S. 2011a. *A Perfect Moral Storm: The Ethical Tragedy of Climate Change*, New York: Oxford University Press.

Gardiner, S. 2011b. "Is No One Responsible for Global Environmental Tragedy? Climate Change as a Challenge to Our Ethical Concepts," in D. Arnold (ed.), *The Ethics of Global Climate Change*, Cambridge: Cambridge University Press.

Garvey, J., 2008. *The Ethics of Climate Change: Right and Wrong in a Warming World*, London/New York: Continuum.

Gaspart, F. and A. Gosseries, 2007. "Are Generational Savings Unjust?" *Politics, Philosophy and Economics* 6(2): 193–217.

Gheaus, A., 2015. "Could There Ever be a Duty to Have Children?" in S. Hannan, S. Brennan, and R. Vernon (eds.), *Permissible Progeny? The Morality of Procreation and Parenting*, Oxford: Oxford University Press.

Gheaus, A., 2016. "The Right to Parent and Duties Concerning Future Generations," *Journal of Political Philosophy* 24 (4): 487–508.

Gonzalez-Ricoy, I., 2020. "Intergenerational Justice and Institutions for the Long Term," in K. Goetz (ed.), *The Oxford Handbook of Time and Politics*, New York: Oxford University Press.

Gonzalez-Ricoy, I. and A. Gosseries (eds.), 2016a. *Institutions for Future Generations*, Oxford: Oxford University Press.

Gonzalez-Ricoy, I. and A. Gosseries, 2016b. "Designing Institutions for Future Generations: An Introduction," in I. Gonzalez-Ricoy and A. Gosseries (eds.), *Institutions for Future Generations*, Oxford: Oxford University Press.

Goodin, R., 1999. "The Sustainability Ethic: Political, Not Just Moral," *Journal of Applied Philosophy* 16(3): 247–54.

Goodin, R., 2000. "Democratic Deliberation Within," *Philosophy and Public Affairs* 29(1): 81–109.

Goodin, R., 2007. "Enfranchising All Affected Interests, and its Alternatives," *Philosophy and Public Affairs* 35(1): 40–68.

Gosseries, A., 2004a. *Penser la Justice entre les Générations: De l'Affaire Perruche à la Réforme des Retraites*, Paris: Aubier-Flammarion.

Gosseries, A., 2004b. "Historical Emissions and Free-Riding," *Ethical Perspectives* 11(1): 36–60.

Gosseries, A., 2008. "On Future Generations' Future Rights," *Journal of Political Philosophy* 16(4): 446–74.

Gosseries, A., 2009. "Three Models of Intergenerational Reciprocity," in A. Gosseries and L. Meyer (eds.), *Intergenerational Justice*, Oxford: Oxford University Press.

Gosseries, A., 2011. "Sufficientarianism," in E. Craig (ed.), *Routledge Encyclopedia of Philosophy Online*, <https://www.rep.routledge.com/articles/thematic/sufficientarianism/v-1>.

Gosseries, A., 2014a. "What Makes Age Discrimination Special?

A Philosophical Look at the ECJ Case Law," *Netherlands Journal of Legal Philosophy* 43(1): 59–80.

Gosseries, A., 2014b. "Nations, Generations and Climate Justice," *Global Policy* 5(1): 96–102.

Gosseries, A., 2014c. "The Intergenerational Case for Constitutional Rigidity," *Ratio Juris* 27(4): 528–39.

Gosseries, A., 2016. "Intergenerational Justice, Sufficiency, and Health," in C. Fourie and A. Rid (eds.), *What is Enough? Sufficiency, Justice, and Health*, Oxford: Oxford University Press.

Gosseries, A., 2019. "Are Inequalities between Us and the Dead Intergenerationally Unjust?" *Critical Review of International Social and Political Philosophy* 22(3): 284–300.

Gosseries, A., 2021. "Can We Rule the Future (and Does it Matter)?" *Rivista di Filosofia del Diritto* 10(2): 285–300.

Gosseries, A., 2022. "Intergenerational Metaphors," in S. Gardiner (ed.), *The Oxford Handbook of Intergenerational Ethics*, New York: Oxford University Press.

Gosseries, A. and L. Meyer (eds.), 2009. *Intergenerational Justice*, Oxford: Oxford University Press.

Gosseries, A. and D. Zwarthoed, 2016. "Generations and Global Justice," in D. Held and P. Maffettone (eds.), *Global Political Theory*, Cambridge: Polity.

Heath, J. 2013. "The Structure of Intergenerational Cooperation," *Philosophy and Public Affairs* 41(1): 31–66.

Heyd, D., 1992. *Genethics: Moral Issues in the Creation of People*, Berkeley/Los Angeles/Oxford: University of California Press.

Hillier, P., 2019. "Millennials? Baby Boomers? Gen Z? Let's Stop with These Nonsense Buzzwords," *The Guardian*, Nov. 5.

Holtug, N., 2002. "The Harm Principle," *Ethical Theory and Moral Practice* 5(4): 357–89.

Howarth, R., 1992. "Intergenerational Justice and the Chain of Obligation," *Environmental Values* 1(2): 133–40.

Jacobs, A., 2011. *Governing for the Long Term: Democracy and the Politics of Investment*, Cambridge: Cambridge University Press.

Jamieson, D., 2010. "Climate Change, Responsibility, and Justice," *Science and Engineering Ethics* 16(3): 431–45.

Johansson, J. and O. Risberg, 2019. "The Preemption Problem," *Philosophical Studies* 176: 351–65.

Jordan, A. et al. 2013. "Going beyond Two Degrees? The Risks and Opportunities of Alternative Options," *Climate Policy* 13(6): 751–69.

Kaczmarek, P. and S. Beard, 2020. "Human Extinction and Our Obligations to the Past," *Utilitas* 32(2): 199–208.

Kahn, P., 1999. *The Human Relationship with Nature: Development and Culture*, Cambridge, MA/London: MIT Press.

Karnein, A., 2016. "Can We Represent Future Generations?," in I. Gonzalez-Ricoy and A. Gosseries (eds.), *Institutions for Future Generations*, Oxford: Oxford University Press.

Knutti, R., J. Rogelj, J. Sedlacek, and E. Fischer, 2015. "A Scientific Critique of the Two-Degree Climate Change Target," *Nature Geoscience* 9: 13–19.

Kohli, M., 2005. "Generational Changes and Generational Equity," in M. Johnson (ed.), *The Cambridge Handbook of Age and Ageing*, Cambridge: Cambridge University Press.

Koskimaa, V. and T. Raunio, 2020. "Encouraging a Longer Time Horizon: The Committee for the Future in the Finnish Eduskunta," *Journal of Legislative Studies* 26(2): 159–79.

Landes, X., 2015. "How Fair is Actuarial Fairness?" *Journal of Business Ethics* 128(3): 519–33.

Laslett, P. and J. Fishkin (eds.), 1992. *Justice between Age Groups and Generations*, New Haven/London: Yale University Press.

Lippert-Rasmussen, K., 2012a. "'Equality of What?' and Intergenerational Justice," *Ethical Perspectives* 19(3): 501–26.

Lippert-Rasmussen, K., 2012b. "Democratic Egalitarianism versus Luck Egalitarianism: What is at Stake?" *Philosophical Topics* 40(1): 117–34.

Loi, M., 2014. "Why a Prohibition on Savings is Illiberal," *Diacritica* 28(2): 289–300.

Lotz, M., 2006. "Feinberg, Mills, and the Child's Right to an Open Future," *Journal of Social Philosophy* 37(4): 537–51.

Luper, S., 2021. "Death," *The Stanford Encyclopedia of Philosophy* (Fall 2021 edn.), E. N. Zalta (ed.), <https://plato.stanford.edu/archives/fall2021/entries/death/>.

MacKenzie, M., 2016. "Institutional Design and the Sources of Short-Termism," in I. Gonzalez-Ricoy and A. Gosseries (eds.), *Institutions for Future Generations*, Oxford: Oxford University Press.

MacKenzie, M., 2021. *Future Publics: Democracy, Deliberation, and Future-Regarding Collective Action*, New York: Oxford University Press.

McKerlie, D., 2012. *Justice between the Young and the Old*, Oxford/New York: Oxford University Press.

McKinnon, C. 2019. "The Panglossian Politics of the Geoclique," *Critical Review of International Social and Political Philosophy* 23(5): 584–99.

Meyer, L., 2004. "Compensating Wrongless Historical Emissions of Greenhouse Gases," *Ethical Perspectives* 11: 22–37.

Meyer, L., 2021. "Intergenerational Justice," *The Stanford Encyclopedia of Philosophy* (Summer 2021 edn.), E. N. Zalta (ed.), <https://plato.stanford.edu/archives/sum2021/entries/justice-intergenerational/>.

Meyer, L. and D. Roser, 2009. "Enough for the Future," in A. Gosseries and L. Meyer (eds.), *Intergenerational Justice*, Oxford: Oxford University Press.

Miller, D., 2009. "Global Justice and Climate Change: How Should Responsibilities be Distributed? Parts I and II," *Tanner Lectures on Human Values* 28: 119–56.

Mills, C., 2003. "The Child's Right to an Open Future?" *Journal of Social Philosophy* 34(4): 499–509.

Millum, J., 2014. "The Foundations of the Child's Right to an Open Future," *Journal of Social Philosophy* 45(4): 522–38.

Moellendorf, D., 2014. *The Moral Challenge of Dangerous Climate Change: Values, Poverty and Policy*, Cambridge: Cambridge University Press.

Moury, C., 2018. *Perceptions of the Portuguese Political Class on Intergenerational Justice*, Lisbon: Gulbenkian Foundation.

Neumayer, E., 2000. "In Defence of Historical Accountability for Greenhouse Gas Emissions," *Ecological Economics* 33: 185–92.

Neumayer, E., 2003. *Weak versus Strong Sustainability: Exploring the Limits of Two Opposing Paradigms*, Cheltenham: Elgar.

Nordhaus, W., 2007. "A Review of the Stern Review on the Economics of Climate Change," *Journal of Economic Literature* 45: 686–702.

Nussbaum, M., 2011. *Creating Capabilities: The Human Development Approach*, Cambridge, MA: Harvard University Press.

O'Neill, J. and M. O'Neill, 2012. *Social Justice and the Future of Flooding Insurance*, Joseph Rowntree Foundation,

<https://www.jrf.org.uk/report/social-justice-and-future-flood-insurance>.

Page, E., 2007. "Intergenerational Justice of What: Welfare, Resources or Capabilities?" *Environmental Politics* 16(3): 453–69.

Page, E., 2012. "Give it up for Climate Change: A Defence of the Beneficiary Pays Principle," *International Theory* 4(2): 300–30.

Parfit, D., 1976. "On Doing the Best for Our Children," in M. D. Bayles (ed.), *Ethics and Population*, Cambridge, MA: Schenkman.

Parfit, D., 1984. *Reasons and Persons*, New York: Oxford University Press.

Perry, S., 2000. "On the Relationship between Corrective and Distributive Justice," in J. Horder (ed.), *Oxford Essays in Jurisprudence*, 4th series, Oxford: Oxford University Press.

Posner, E. and D. Weisbach, 2010. *Climate Change Justice*, Princeton/Oxford: Princeton University Press.

Povitkina, M., 2018. "The Limits of Democracy in Tackling Climate Change," *Environmental Politics* 27(3): 411–32.

Randalls, S. 2010. "History of the 2 °C Climate Target," *WIREs Climate Change* 1: 598–605.

Ramsey, F., 1928. "A Mathematical Theory of Saving," *Economic Journal* 38: 543–59.

Rawls, J., 1971. *A Theory of Justice*, Cambridge, MA: Belknap Press.

Rey, A. (ed.), 2012. *Dictionnaire Historique de la Langue Française* (vol. 1), Paris: Le Robert.

Risse, M., 2005. "How Does the Global Order Harm the Poor?" *Philosophy and Public Affairs*, 33(4): 349–76.

Risse, M., 2012. *Global Justice*, Princeton/London: Princeton University Press.

Roberts, M., 1998. *Child versus Childmaker: Future Persons and Present Duties in Ethics and the Law*, Lanham/Oxford: Rowman and Littlefield.

Robeyns, I., 2017. *Wellbeing, Freedom and Social Justice: The Capability Approach Re-Examined*, Cambridge: Open Book.

Roemer, J., 2011. "The Ethics of Intertemporal Distribution in a Warming Planet," *Environmental and Resource Economics* 48: 363–90.

Rose, M., 2019. "All-Affected, Non-Identity and the Political Representation of Future Generations: Linking Intergenerational Justice with Democracy," in T. Cottier, S. Lalani, and C. Siziba (eds.), *Intergenerational Equity: Environmental and Cultural Concerns*, Leiden/Boston: Brill Nijhoff.

Sagoff, M., 1988. *The Economy of the Earth*, Cambridge: Cambridge University Press.

Scheffler, S., 2018. *Why Worry about Future Generations?* New York: Oxford University Press.

Sen, A., 1992. *Inequality Reexamined*, Oxford: Clarendon Press.

Shields, L., 2016. *Just Enough: Sufficiency as a Demand of Justice*, Edinburgh: Edinburgh University Press.

Shiffrin, S., 1999. "Wrongful Life, Procreative Responsibility, and the Significance of Harm," *Legal Theory* 5(2): 117–48.

Shue, H., 2022. *The Pivotal Generation: Why We Have a Moral Responsibility to Slow Climate Change Right Now*, Princeton: Princeton University Press.

Slemrod, J., 1986. "Saving and the Fear of Nuclear War," *Journal of Conflict Resolution* 30(3): 403–19.

Smith, G., 2020. "Enhancing the Legitimacy of Offices for Future Generations: The Case for Public Participation," *Political Studies* 68(4): 996–1013.

Smith, G., 2021. *Can Democracy Safeguard the Future?* Cambridge: Polity.

Solow, R., 1974. "Intergenerational Equity and Exhaustible Resources," *Review of Economic Studies* 41: 29–45.

Stern, N., 2007. *The Economics of Climate Change: The Stern Review*, Cambridge: Cambridge University Press.

Uhuru Bidadanure, J., 2021. *Justice across Ages: Treating Young and Old as Equals*, New York/Oxford: Oxford University Press.

Vandeschrick, C., 2001. "The Lexis Diagram, a Misnomer," *Demographic Research* 4(3): 95–124.

Van Parijs, P., 2001. "Difference Principles," in S. Freeman (ed.), *The Cambridge Companion to John Rawls*, Cambridge: Cambridge University Press.

Wade-Benzoni, K. A., 2002. "A Golden Rule over Time: Reciprocity in Intergenerational Allocation Decisions," *Academy of Management Journal* 45(5): 1011–28.

Ward, H., 2008. "Liberal Democracy and Sustainability," *Environmental Politics* 17(3): 386–409.

WCED (World Commission on Environment and Development), 1987. *Our Common Future.* Oxford: Oxford University Press.

White, J., 2013. "Thinking Generations," *British Journal of Sociology* 64(2): 216–47.

Wilson, E. O., 2016. *Half-Earth: Our Planet's Fight for Life*, New York: Norton.

Woodward, J., 1986. "The Non-Identity Problem," *Ethics* 96: 804–31.

Wurster, S., 2013. "Comparing Ecological Sustainability in Autocracies and Democracies," *Contemporary Politics* 19(1): 76–93.

Zwarthoed, D., 2015. "Creating Frugal Citizens: The Liberal Case for Teaching Frugality," *Theory and Research in Education* 13(3): 286–307.

Index